W9-AMY-102

Sustaining
Earth's
Energy Resources

ENVIRONMENT AT RISK

Sustaining Earth's
Energy Resources

ANN HEINRICHS

Marshall Cavendish
Benchmark
New York

Other Marshall Cavendish Offices:
Marshall Cavendish International (Asia) Private Limited, 1 New Industrial Road, Singapore 536196 • Marshall Cavendish International (Thailand) Co Ltd. 253 Asoke, 12th Flr, Sukhumvit 21 Road, Klongtoey Nua, Wattana, Bangkok 10110, Thailand • Marshall Cavendish (Malaysia) Sdn Bhd, Times Subang, Lot 46, Subang Hi-Tech Industrial Park, Batu Tiga, 40000 Shah Alam, Selangor Darul Ehsan, Malaysia

Marshall Cavendish is a trademark of Times Publishing Limited

All websites were available and accurate when this book was sent to press.

Library of Congress Cataloging-in-Publication Data
Heinrichs, Ann.
Sustaining Earth's energy resources / by Ann Heinrichs.
p. cm. — (Environment at risk)
Includes bibliographical references and index.
Summary: "Provides comprehensive information on Earth's sources of renewable and nonrenewable energy, how they are used, their benefits and disadvantages, their interrelationships with the natural world, and the future of Earth's sources of energy"—Provided by publisher.
ISBN 978-0-7614-4007-9
1. Renewable energy sources—Juvenile literature. 2. Power resources—Environmental aspects—Juvenile literature. 3. Energy development—Environmental aspects—Juvenile literature. I. Title.
TJ808.2.H45 2011
333.79—dc22

Editor: Christine Florie
Publisher: Michelle Bisson
Art Director: Anahid Hamparian
Series Designer: Sonia Chaghatzbanian

Expert Reader: Dr. Mel Manalis, Environmental Studies, University of California at Santa Barbara

Photo research by Marybeth Kavanagh
Cover photo by Bill Ross/Corbis

The photographs in this book are used by permission and through the courtesy of:
Getty Images: Robert Postma, 2–3; Don Farrall, 2; Maremagnum, 6; Guy Edwardes, 12; Richard du Toit, 9; Steve Allen, 13, 34; Jason Edwards/National Geographic, 14, 36; Ulet Ifansasti, 24; David McNew, 27; David Woodfall, 31; Time & Life Pictures, 43; Christian Science Monitor, 60; Max Alexander, 61; Rebecca Emery/Image Bank, 65; Ethan Miller, 66; Scott Olson, 74; Thomas Del Brase/Stone, 84; Robert Francis, 86; Justin Sullivan, 91; *Photoedit, Inc.*: Phil McCarten, 21; Bonnie Kamin, 95; *The Image Works*: Monika Graff, 22; Michael Siluk, 57; Bob Daemmrich, 69; John Berry/Syracuse Newspapers, 77; Jim West, 80; *Alamy*: blphoto, 38; GmbH & Co.KG, 40; *Corbis*: Historical Picture Archive, 46; Peter Ginter/Science Faction, 59; *AP Images*: Joe Cavaretta, 48; Xinhua, Du Huaju, 50; *AnimalsAnimals-Earth Scenes*: Kent, Breck P., 52

Printed in Malaysia (T)
1 3 5 6 4 2

Contents

One

Energy Resources:
A Global Challenge

Catch a ride home on a blustery winter day. Walk in the door, and you relish the warmth of your cozy home. Switch on the lights, go to the refrigerator, heat up a snack in the microwave, cruise the Internet, listen to some music, call a friend, flip on the TV, take a hot shower, and snuggle into bed.

Without even thinking about it, you just consumed a lot of energy and burned a lot of fuel. Every day about 29 pounds (13 kilograms) of coal are burned to generate all the electrical energy one person uses. That adds up to more than 5 tons of coal a year. Then look at the energy you use for transportation. Every year the average U.S. resident uses 500 gallons (1,892 liters) of gasoline.

You are just one person with energy needs. Imagine how much energy everyone in your neighborhood and your city consumes. Now picture the whole world, with a population of

Every day, vast amounts of energy are consumed around the world. In Hong Kong, China, energy is needed for transportation and for lighting up the cityscape.

more than 6 billion and growing. All these people need energy to cook, travel, light their homes, and carry on their industries. Where does all that energy come from? Will there be enough energy to go around? Can our planet survive infinite energy consumption? These are important issues that today face scientists, governments, and ordinary citizens worldwide.

What Is Energy?

Energy is defined as the ability to do work. It may be the ability to move, lift, or push something or the ability to produce heat or light. Energy lights up your room, gets you to school, cooks your pizza, plays your favorite shows and tunes, and enables you to think and move.

People once relied on the muscle power of humans and animals to do work. They walked to get somewhere, and animals carried their loads. Natural energy resources worked for them, too. The sun dried their foods and hides, wind and water moved their boats, and wood fueled their fires.

Today, life is much more complex. We need to get a lot more work done. We need to travel far and fast, send and receive information quickly, stay comfortable in varying climates, see in the dark, preserve food for long periods, and make millions of intricate devices. Sheer muscle power and the simple effects of nature are not sufficient to do such a massive amount of work. That is why we need a vast array of energy resources.

Forms of Energy

Energy comes in many forms. Radiant energy is light, and thermal energy is heat. An object in motion has mechanical energy. Broccoli, flashlight batteries, and gasoline are some things that store chemical energy. All forms of energy are grouped into two broad categories: potential energy and kinetic energy. Potential energy is stored energy, while kinetic energy is moving energy. Take a roller coaster car, for example. When it pauses just before making a drop, it has potential energy. That energy quickly changes to kinetic energy when the car goes careening down the slope.

This kind of change follows the law of conservation of energy. It states that energy can be neither created nor destroyed, but it can be transformed or converted from one form to another. We take advantage of this when we convert one form of energy into a form that can do work for us. For example, when we burn wood, its chemical energy is transformed into thermal and radiant energy (heat and light).

Renewable and Nonrenewable Resources

Renewable energy is energy derived from natural resources that can be replenished, or replaced, through natural processes. Renewable resources such as solar, wind, water, biomass, and geothermal energy cannot be used up. No matter how much we use them, the sun will keep shining, winds will blow, rain will fall, plants will grow, and Earth will emit heat.

Nonrenewable resources, on the other hand, cannot be replaced naturally. Even though plentiful supplies may exist, they can be used up. One example is uranium, the major source of fuel for the reactors that create nuclear energy.

Coal is a nonrenewable source of energy. It takes millions of years to be created. Here, tons of ore are mined near Witbank, South Africa.

Thermodynamics: The Laws of Energy

Thermodynamics is the study of energy transformation. It is the science underlying all studies of how we use energy to do work. Thermodynamics follows certain basic principles, or laws, that define how energy does and does not behave. These laws apply to all forms of energy, including heat energy, chemical energy, and electrical energy.

The first law of thermodynamics is also known as the law of conservation of energy. It states that the total amount of energy in a closed system does not change. Energy can be transformed from one type to another, but it can never be created or destroyed. So when you put muffins in the oven to bake, the oven's heat energy is transferred to the muffins, triggering the chemical energy that makes the muffins rise.

The second law of thermodynamics gets more specific about the direction energy conversion follows. This law can be stated in many ways. One is that heat can never flow from a cooler object to a warmer one. Rather, heat will flow from a hot object to a cool object until the two reach equilibrium, or have equal temperatures. So, if you put a hot muffin in a cool container, the muffin will heat the air in the container until the muffin and the air are the same temperature.

Another way of stating the second law is this: in any energy conversion, there is less energy available to do work after the conversion than before it. The longer the muffin exudes heat, the less heat energy is available within the container (unless you add heat from outside). The amount of energy remains the same, but less of it is available to do the work of heating.

This "unavailability" is called entropy. Entropy has been variously defined as dispersal, dissipation, degradation, randomness, disorder, and chaos. Entropy increases over time, and this process is irreversible.

In terms of energy conservation, you want to minimize entropy and maximize the energy available to do work. That means using systems that generate energy as efficiently as possible.

Sunlight: The Ultimate Energy Resource

Sunlight is the most basic energy resource on the planet. Plants absorb sunlight, or radiant energy from the Sun—also known as solar energy. They transform that energy into sugars and starches, which they break down to create chemical energy. This process is called photosynthesis, from the Greek words for "light" and "placing together." Directly or indirectly, all life on Earth depends on this process. Farther up the food chain, animals and humans convert plants' chemical energy into the energy to stay alive and function.

Fossil fuels—coal, petroleum, and natural gas—are nonrenewable as well. Formed over millions of years, they can be replenished in millions more years. Therefore, for all practical purposes, they cannot be replaced.

Power Plants and Distribution Grids

Most power plants have turbines and generators. A turbine is a machine with rotating blades that spin around like the blades of a fan. Some turbines are turned by wind or water, while others are turned by steam. In thermal power plants, a fuel such as coal is burned to heat water and produce steam. The steam then turns the turbines. A turbine's central shaft is connected to a generator. As the turbine spins, the generator transforms the mechanical energy of the spinning shaft into electricity.

Electricity travels from the power plant to homes and businesses through a network called the power distribution grid. In this system electric power goes from the generators

The energy in this steam-powered turbine is transformed into electricity.

13

High-voltage power lines carry electricity for miles across the Namibian Desert in Africa.

to a transmission substation. The substation's transformers increase the electricity's voltage, or electrical energy potential, for transmission over long distances. From there the electricity travels along high-voltage power lines strung between tall steel towers. (In some cases the electricity travels over underground lines.) These power lines run to populated areas, where they enter another substation. Its transformers convert the high-voltage electricity to a lower voltage for customers' use. From the substation, power lines carry the electricity to homes, factories, and other businesses.

Electricity can travel hundreds of miles over a distribution grid. Thus, it can reach customers who live far from a power plant. Electricity generated by wind, solar, and other resources can hook up to the grid, too. They add renewable energy to a community's existing power system.

Measuring Energy

Energy is measured in several ways. The most basic unit for measuring energy is the joule. The joule has a rather complex scientific definition, but there is a simple way to picture it. One

14

Table 1. Electric Power Measurements

Symbol	Unit	Definition	Common Usage
W	watt	Production/use of 1 joule of energy per second	lightbulbs, household appliances
kW	kilowatt	1,000 watts	electric heaters, engines, machines
MW	megawatt	1 million (10^6) watts	output capacity of electric power plants
GW	gigawatt	1 billion (10^9) watts	output capacity of large electric power plants
TW	terawatt	1 trillion (10^{12}) watts	large-scale energy figures, such as worldwide usage
kWh	kilowatt hours	Energy consumed by using 1 kW of power for 1 hour	energy usage by consumers (households, businesses)
MWh	megawatt hours	Energy consumed by using 1 MW of power for 1 hour	energy usage by large-scale consumers; a power plant's daily output

joule is the amount of energy required to lift a 1-pound (0.45-kg) object 9 inches (22.9 centimeters). Measuring *energy* is not the same as measuring *power*. Power includes a time element. It is the rate at which energy is produced or used over a given period of time. Power is measured in terms of the watt (W). One watt of power is equal to 1 joule of energy per second.

Electric power plants are usually rated in terms of megawatts (MW), or millions of watts. This rating tells how much electric power they can produce when operating at their peak. A 1,000-MW power plant is capable of generating a maximum of 1,000 MW of electricity, or 1 billion watts of power per second. However, no power plants operate at peak capacity all the time. Consumers use more electricity at certain times of the day and year and less at other times. Power plants regularly shut down for maintenance, too.

Watts are also used to rate electrical devices. A 100-watt lightbulb uses 100 watts of energy, and a small hair dryer might use 1,000 watts, or 1 kilowatt (kW). To figure out how much electrical energy you are using, you must factor in the length of time you are using it. For example, if you burn that lightbulb for ten hours or use that hair dryer for one hour, you are using 1 kilowatt hour (kWh) of electricity. Electric companies usually bill their customers by the number of kilowatt hours they use during a given period.

Another measure of energy is the British thermal unit (BTU). It is defined as the amount of heat needed to raise the temperature of 1 pound (0.45 kg) of water 1 degree Fahrenheit (0.56 degree Celsius). BTUs are used to measure how much heat energy a fuel can generate. Coal, for example, contains on average about 13 to 24 million BTUs per ton, depending on the quality of the coal. In terms of watts, the average ton of coal generates about 2,000 kilowatt hours of electricity.

BTUs are also used to rate the power of heating and cooling equipment such as stoves and air conditioners. A small air conditioner might be rated at 5,000 BTUs (meaning 5,000 BTUs per hour), while a larger, more powerful one could rate 20,000 BTUs or more. Relating BTUs to watts, using 5,000 BTUs of power an hour requires about 1.5 kilowatt hours of electrical energy.

A Brief History of Energy Consumption

From the time prehistoric humans gathered around blazing fires up until the recent past, wood was humans' major fuel. By burning wood, people could generate energy to keep warm and cook food. Gradually, humans invented machines to do work for them. Devices such as windmills and waterwheels harnessed wind and water power to provide the energy for tasks such as grinding grain. Humans also started using animals to do work and provide transportation.

As late as the 1700s animals were providing humans with the energy for transportation, and tasks such as weaving cloth and making tools were done by hand. That began to change with the Industrial Revolution of the late 1700s, a major turning point in human history. The revolution marked the transition from manual labor to machine-based manufacturing. Starting in England, it quickly spread throughout Europe, the United States, and the rest of the world.

The revolution began with a rapid increase in the number of textile mills, or cloth factories, using waterwheels to power complex machinery. Coal soon replaced water power as the Industrial Revolution's major energy source. In the late 1700s the Scottish engineer James Watt (1736–1819) developed an efficient steam engine. It involved burning coal to boil water into steam that would drive machinery. In time coal-burning steam engines powered factories, ironworks, water pumps, steamboats, and railroad locomotives. By about 1885 coal had replaced wood as the major fuel consumed in the United States.

Water power made a comeback in the 1880s, when engineers found that falling water could generate electricity in hydroelectric plants. However, coal-fired power plants remained the major source of U.S. electric power. When the mass production of automobiles began in the early 1900s, another fossil fuel began its rise as an energy source—petroleum. Natural gas was also found to be a good fuel for cooking, heating, and generating electricity. By 1947 Americans were consuming more petroleum and natural gas than coal. Within about thirty-five years the consumption of petroleum and natural gas quadrupled. So many cars and trucks

Table 2. Major Sources of U.S. Electric Power, 2008

Source	Percentage	Totals
Coal	48.5%	Fossil fuels 71.9%
Other fossil fuels (petroleum, natural gas, other gases)	23.4%	
Nuclear power	19.2%	Nuclear 19.2%
Hydroelectric power	6.1%	Renewables 8.8%
Other renewable sources (biomass, wind, geothermal, solar)	2.7%	

Note: Figures do not add up to 100 percent due to rounding.

Source: U.S. Department of Energy, Energy Information Administration, Net Generation by Energy Source, Total (all sectors), October 28, 2008, http://www.eia.doe.gov/cheaf/electricity/epm/table1_1.html (accessed 14 November 2008).

needed fuel that the United States began importing petroleum from other countries. Meanwhile, nuclear power had arrived on the scene. The tremendous energy released by splitting uranium atoms was put to work generating electricity.

By the 1970s the consumption of energy resources was becoming a major issue around the world. As populations grew and industrial development escalated, so did the demand for coal for electricity and petroleum for transportation fuel. Gradually, citizens and governments alike awakened to three realities: (1) fossil fuels have harmful effects on the environment worldwide; (2) supplies of these fuels are limited; and (3) most industrialized nations have to import fuels from other countries. This led to the search for alternative energy resources that are clean, renewable, and readily available. That quest has become one of the major global challenges of the twenty-first century.

Two
Fossil Fuels:
Millions of Years
in the Making

Fossil fuels are remnants from a long-lost prehistoric time. They are called fossil fuels because they were formed from the remains of plants and animals that lived hundreds of millions of years ago. Although there are a few others, the three major fossil fuels are coal, petroleum, and natural gas. (Petroleum is often called oil.)

Most fossil fuels originated in a time long before dinosaurs roamed the planet. Fossil fuels were mainly formed during a time called the Carboniferous Period, more than 300 million years ago. That period is named for carbon, a key component of all living things and the major element in fossil fuels. Carbon that sustained life millions of years ago is still with us today in forms such as carbon dioxide (CO_2).

Greenhouse Gases and Climate Change

The United States is the world's largest consumer of fossil fuels. Coal, oil, and natural gas provide more than 70 percent of U.S. energy needs. That includes almost two-thirds of U.S.

Greenhouse gases are emitted into the atmosphere every day. This cement mixer spews noxious gases on its way to a construction site.

electric power and almost all of U.S. transportation fuels. When we burn these fuels, CO_2 and other gases are released into the atmosphere.

Green plants naturally absorb CO_2 and release oxygen through the process of photosynthesis. For thousands of years plants could process the CO_2 that humans produced through such activities as burning wood. But now, however, vehicles and industries discharge so much CO_2 that no amount of vegetation can absorb it all. Tons of CO_2 hang in the atmosphere, encircling the earth and trapping heat close to the surface. Because the glass walls of a greenhouse trap heat in much the same way, this is called the greenhouse effect.

About 84 percent of greenhouse gases are CO_2. The rest include methane, nitrous oxide, and sulfur compounds. Naturally occurring greenhouse gases keep the planet from being too cold to support life. Today, however, most scientists believe that the sheer overload of greenhouse gases is contributing to climate change and global warming worldwide.

Emissions and Climate Change

Former U.S. vice president Al Gore (below) wrote and starred in the 2006 documentary film *An Inconvenient Truth.* Its message is that human activities are intensifying global warming by polluting the atmosphere with carbon dioxide and other greenhouse gases. Unless these emissions are drastically reduced, says Gore, the effects will be catastrophic. One effect, for example, is the melting of ice in Greenland, Antarctica, and the north polar ice cap. Continued melting could cause sea levels to rise, devastating coastal areas worldwide. Although a few scientists say global warming is a myth made up by alarmists, most climate experts agree with the inconvenient facts about global warming. Gore and a team of scientists called the Intergovernmental Panel on Climate Change were awarded the 2007 Nobel Peace Prize for their work.

Almost everywhere you look, something is sending out greenhouse gases. The United States emitted about 7.8 billion tons (7.1 billion metric tons) of those gases in 2006. Some came from industrial sites, such as factories and mines. Some came from the exhaust from cars, trucks, buses, airplanes, and other vehicles. Commercial buildings such as bookstores, shopping malls, schools, hotels, and office buildings also give off emissions. Your own home is probably responsible for emitting greenhouse gases, too. If your electricity comes from a coal-fired power plant, you are burning coal whenever you use electricity. However, petroleum is the major source of CO_2 and other greenhouse gases. In 2006, 44 percent of U.S. greenhouse-gas emissions came from petroleum.

From Prehistoric Seas to Your Gas Tank

Petroleum was formed from the creatures and plants that lived in prehistoric lakes and seas. When these organisms died, they sank to the bottom, decomposed, and were covered with layer after layer of mud, rock, and sand. Over millions of years this material was buried and then subjected to intense pressure and heat. This brought about chemical changes that transformed the material into the black liquid called petroleum.

Petroleum can contain hundreds of types of hydrocarbon molecules—chains of carbon and hydrogen atoms in different arrangements and lengths. When petroleum is first pumped out of the ground, it is called crude oil. At an oil refinery the crude oil is heated, and the different hydrocarbons are separated out. Some are gases such as methane, propane, and butane. Others are liquids, including kerosene, home heating oil, diesel fuel, and gasoline. Then there are thick oils and greases such as motor oil, and finally, solids such as asphalt, tar, and paraffin (wax).

In the case of gasoline and diesel fuel, tanker trucks carry them to gas stations, where people can fill up their gas tanks. Most vehicles have an internal-combustion engine that converts the gasoline's chemical energy into mechanical energy, making the vehicle go. By-products of this process flow out of the tailpipe and into the atmosphere. These emissions include

When petroleum is first pumped from the ground, it is called crude oil (above). Later, it is refined into its separate components for various uses.

CO_2, carbon monoxide, nitrogen oxides, sulfur dioxide, and various hydrocarbons.

Petroleum: Supply and Demand

Saudi Arabia is the world's largest oil producer, followed by Russia, the United States, Iran, China, Mexico, and Canada. The United States is the world's largest consumer of petroleum, accounting for almost one-fourth of the world's consumption. Americans use almost 21 million barrels of oil every day. (A barrel is equal to 42 U.S. gallons, or 159 liters.) The next-largest consumers are China, Japan, Russia, Germany, and India.

Even though the United States is a major oil producer, it imports more than 10 million barrels of oil a day. Many Americans believe that those imports come mostly from Middle Eastern countries, but that is not the case. Canada is the country's largest supplier of imported oil, followed by Saudi Arabia, Mexico, Venezuela, and Nigeria.

Petroleum is a nonrenewable resource because it cannot be replaced. Most people agree on this, but there the agreement ends. Some people say a huge supply of oil remains in the ground, including the reserves we know about and those yet to be found. The only obstacles to getting it out of the ground are environmental regulations and government approval.

Others say the days of plentiful oil are over, citing a concept called peak oil. Peak oil is the point at which world oil production reaches its peak, followed by an inevitable decline. Although opinions vary about when this point will come, or whether it has come already, many oil experts agree with the concept. The world is already consuming more oil than it produces. Production costs are rising as oil becomes harder to find. With the growth in world population, oil consumption will continue to increase as well.

Cleaner Fuels, Cleaner Cars

In the early 1900s many U.S. carmakers manufactured electric automobiles. Chugging along at speeds up to 20 miles (32 kilometers) per hour, electric cars were popular among upper-class folks for taking casual spins around town.

Then, in 1908, the mass-produced, gasoline-powered Ford Model T appeared. By the 1920s, as Ford's assembly-line production improved, a Model T could be had for less than $300. Whizzing by at up to 45 miles (72 km) an hour, it was great for long-distance road trips, too. This affordable vehicle became the car of choice for middle-class families.

Most cars made since then have run on gasoline. Now, in the search for alternative fuels, ethanol and biodiesel are welcomed as clean, renewable alternatives to gasoline (see chapter 7). Natural gas is sometimes used as a substitute for gasoline, too (see p. 28). In addition, many new types of cars using alternative fuels are either on the market or in development. Thus, electric cars are making a comeback.

Today's electric vehicles run on the electric energy stored in a battery pack. Depending on the model, they can run from 40 miles (64 km) up to about 150 miles (241 km) before the battery needs to be recharged. Recharging can take anywhere from a few minutes to a few hours. Drivers can recharge the battery pack at an electrical outlet at home or at a charging station. Electric cars give off no harmful emissions, although the electricity needed for recharging the batteries may come from coal-fired power plants that burn fossil fuels.

Hydrogen vehicles are another alternative. Some burn hydrogen gas as a fuel in the same way gasoline-powered vehicles do. A more fuel-efficient type of hydrogen vehicle has an electric motor that runs on hydrogen fuel cells. A hydrogen fuel cell contains hydrogen and oxygen under high pressure. The two elements interact, producing electricity and water. The electricity powers the motor, while water or water vapor is ejected as an emission. To produce enough power to run a vehicle, many fuel cells are connected in a fuel-cell stack. Several U.S. and foreign companies are making hydrogen cars today.

Hybrid-electric vehicles (HEV) use a combination of gasoline and electric power. They have higher fuel efficiency and emit less pollution than gasoline-powered vehicles. The Toyota Prius, introduced in Japan in 1997, was the first mass-produced HEV. Since then many other car manufacturers have released hybrid models. A variety of other alternative-fuel vehicles are currently

Take the Hydrogen Highway

Where can you fill up your hydrogen car? Just pull up to a station along a hydrogen highway—a network of hydrogen filling stations along a stretch of highway. These stations enable drivers of hydrogen vehicles to travel long distances without running out of fuel. The California Hydrogen Highway stretches along the state's west coast. As of 2008 it had twenty-six hydrogen stations in operation and more in the planning stages. Florida and New York State are planning hydrogen highways, too. These highways are a step toward creating an infrastructure that supports clean, renewable fuels.

under development, and researchers are trying to find ways to make them affordable.

Natural Gas

Natural gas is formed from the same materials as petroleum, and the two are often found in the same underground deposits. Natural gas is composed mainly of methane gas, with other components such as ethane, propane, and butane gases. It is a major fuel for producing electricity in power plants. Today, most newer gas-fired plants use the combined-cycle process. They burn natural gas to generate electricity while recovering waste heat to make steam for creating additional electricity. Natural gas is also piped into homes as a cooking and heating fuel. Many industries around the world use natural gas as their energy source, too.

In 2006, 20 percent of U.S. greenhouse gas emissions came from natural gas. Still, compared to oil and coal, gas is a relatively clean fuel, producing much less CO_2 when it burns than other fossil fuels. This makes natural gas an attractive alternative fuel for vehicles. Today, millions of natural-gas vehicles (NGVs) are in operation worldwide.

Liquefied natural gas (LNG) is one form of vehicle fuel. It is natural gas that has been cooled to an extremely low temperature to condense it to liquid form. LNG is used mostly to fuel buses, garbage trucks, long-distance trucks, and other heavy-duty vehicles.

Compressed natural gas (CNG) is another alternative fuel. It is natural gas condensed under high pressure and often stored in metal cylinders. A growing number of trucks, buses, and trains are running on CNG. As for passenger cars, the Honda Civic GX was the only U.S. car running on pure CNG as of 2008. Cars can also be converted into bi-fuel vehicles that use a combination of gasoline and CNG. Common in Europe, bi-fuel cars are beginning to capture the interest of U.S. drivers.

Coal

Unlike oil and gas, coal was formed only from plants. Coal production began 300 to 400 million years ago as decayed

Table 1. How Much Coal Are You Burning Today?

Device	Length of use	Amount of coal consumed
100-watt lightbulb	24 hours a day for 1 year	877 pounds (398 kg)
Refrigerator	1 year	0.5 tons
Stove	1 year	0.5 tons
Hot water heater	1 year	2 tons

Sources: U.S. Department of Energy, Energy Information Administration, "Coal Demand," October 2008, http://www.eia.doe.gov/neic/infosheets/coaldemand.html (accessed 14 November 2008); DOE, "Coal: Our Most Abundant Fuel," http://fossil.energy.gov/education/energylessons/coal/gen_coal.html (accessed 14 August 2008).

trees, gigantic ferns, and other vegetation died in prehistoric swamps. Depending on the length of time this material was buried and compressed, it formed different substances. The youngest, least transformed material is called peat, a spongy material that has not yet become coal. In some places people burn peat to heat their homes. The next four layers are different grades of coal.

First comes lignite, a soft, brownish-black coal that gives off a small amount of heat when burned. Most of the world's coal reserves consist of lignite. Next is the dull black subbituminous coal. It gives off more heat than lignite. Bituminous coal, often called soft coal, is next. Finally, the most thoroughly transformed layer is anthracite coal. It is the hardest type of coal, and it gives off a great amount of heat when it burns.

Coal is the United States' most abundant fossil fuel. About one-fourth of all known coal reserves—more than any other country in the world—are in the United States. Coal is mined in twenty-six of the fifty states, from Pennsylvania and the Appalachian region through the Midwest and several western states. Mostly used to generate electricity, coal produces about half the electric power in the United States. In coal-fired power plants, it is burned to heat water into steam. That steam drives turbines that power electric generators.

Dirty Coal, Clean Coal

In 2006, 36 percent of U.S. greenhouse gas emissions came from coal. In the burning process the coal's carbon combines with oxygen to form CO_2, which is released into the atmosphere. Impurities such as sulfur dioxide (SO_2) and nitrogen oxides are released, too. They combine with the water droplets in clouds to form sulfuric and nitric acids. Those acids fall back to the earth in what is called acid rain. Acid rain damages forest trees and, in lakes and streams, affects fish, shellfish, and other aquatic life. It also damages stone buildings and monuments, as well as the paint on vehicles.

Burning coal has so many harmful effects that some people suggest eliminating coal-fired power plants altogether. Others suggest cleaning up the process by employing so-called

The destruction from acid rain can be seen on these trees near a petrochemical plant.

clean coal technologies. One method is gasification, in which the coal is converted to synthesis gas, or syngas. Syngas, composed of carbon monoxide and hydrogen, is then burned to generate electricity. This process releases less carbon dioxide than burning coal. Another method, called coal washing, involves crushing and washing the coal with a liquid to remove impurities before burning it.

Other methods treat the flue gas—the smoke rising up the smokestack—after the coal has burned. For example, scrubber systems use water, steam, or absorbent minerals to remove SO_2 and other pollutants from the flue gases. Another method, carbon capture, involves drawing CO_2 out of the flue gases. After that comes the problem of carbon sequestration, or storage—that is, where to put the CO_2. Choices include injecting it deep underground or into the oceans.

Each of these technologies solves one or two pollution issues while leaving others unresolved or creating new problems. Most of these processes are too expensive, too

inefficient, or too risky to be workable on a large scale. That is why many scientists and environmentalists say there is no such thing as clean coal. They also point out that coal mining damages natural areas and that more fossil fuels are burned in transporting the coal to power plants. Nevertheless, with the increase in state and national pollution regulations, researchers continue to work on ways to clean up coal-fired power plant emissions efficiently and affordably.

Three
Nuclear Power: Splitting the Atom

On a cold December morning in 1942 the physicist Enrico Fermi and his colleagues gathered on a squash court beneath the bleachers at the University of Chicago's football field. Filling the court was a huge pile of blocks composed of tons of uranium and other materials. Fermi knew that uranium atoms could be split, releasing unstable, radioactive atoms and energy. Today he hoped to trigger a continuous chain reaction of splitting atoms, releasing a huge quantity of energy, and then make the reaction stop.

This was a risky experiment. If Fermi couldn't control the reaction, the atoms could split all at once, blowing up half the city. At 9:45 AM Fermi gave the signal to begin the test. Gradually he removed the safety controls—metal rods that absorbed the energetic particles from the unstable uranium. This allowed those particles to hit other uranium atoms, making them split as well. Over the next few hours the clicking sounds from Fermi's instruments grew more and more frequent, indicating that more and more atoms were splitting.

By 3:25 PM, splitting atoms were firing particles that split other atoms. A chain reaction was in full swing. Fermi let it continue for twenty-eight minutes. Then, reinserting the safety control rods, he shut down the reaction. Fermi had produced the first controlled nuclear chain reaction. He had split the atom without creating a massive explosion.

Fermi's experiment was part of the Manhattan Project. Its purpose was to develop a nuclear weapon, or atomic bomb, during World War II (1939–1945). Thanks to Fermi and other scientists, the project was a success. In August 1945 the United States dropped the world's first atomic bombs on Hiroshima and Nagasaki, Japan. Within days Japan surrendered, ending the war.

Generating Electricity Around the World

After the war attention turned to finding peaceful uses for nuclear power. The former Soviet Union built the first commercial nuclear power station in 1954. The following year the town of Arco, Idaho, became the first U.S. town powered by nuclear energy. England opened its first nuclear power plant in 1956. And in 1957 Shippingport Atomic Power Station in Beaver County, Pennsylvania, became the first full-scale nuclear power plant in the United States.

Worldwide, nuclear power plants generate about 16 percent of the world's electricity. This nuclear power plant is located in northwest England.

Today, nuclear energy is a significant source of power worldwide. As of 2008 nuclear power provided 16 percent of the world's electricity and 19 percent of the electricity in the United States. The United States has the greatest number of nuclear power plants, with 104. Next in line are France, Japan, and Russia.

Nuclear power is clearly on the rise, but it is a controversial energy resource. Many people are concerned about the safety of nuclear power plants, the danger of accidents, and the disposal of nuclear wastes. Others point out that nuclear fuels could fall into the hands of people who want to make nuclear weapons. As international hostilities escalate, the mass devastation of nuclear warfare is a terrifying prospect. Because of this Germany, Spain, and several other European countries have decided to phase out their nuclear power programs. At the same time, many countries are looking to increase their nuclear capabilities. These include Canada, China, India, Iran, Russia, Japan, and the United States.

How Does Nuclear Power Work?

Nuclear energy is derived from the energy locked inside the nucleus, or center, of an atom. Atoms are made up of three types of particles—protons and neutrons, which form the nucleus, and electrons, which orbit around the nucleus. Most nuclear power plants produce energy by inducing a reaction called nuclear fission. It involves firing a neutron into the nucleus of an atom, splitting the atom apart. This releases a tremendous amount of energy in the form of heat and light. Nuclear fission is the reaction Enrico Fermi controlled in his 1942 experiment. He used uranium, which is still the chemical element most commonly used as fuel in nuclear power plants.

When the nucleus splits, free neutrons are released. Those free neutrons in turn strike other nuclei, creating a chain reaction. In a nuclear weapon, that chain reaction takes place in a split second at an uncontrolled rate, releasing an immense amount of energy and causing mass destruction. In nuclear power plants, however, the chain reaction is controlled within a device called a nuclear reactor. The speed of the

This diagram illustrates the process of nuclear fission, in which a neutron splits an atom apart, producing energy and releasing more neutrons.

reaction is slowed with control rods, or metal rods that absorb some of the energy. Within the reactor, nuclear fission generates heat, which boils water into steam. That steam drives turbines, which in turn power electric generators.

Two types of reactors are used in the United States. In boiling water reactors (BWRs) the heat directly boils water into steam that turns the turbines. About 70 percent of U.S. reactors are pressurized water reactors (PWRs). In this type water heated by the reactor is kept under pressure so it doesn't boil. Instead, it runs through tubes submerged in freshwater that boils into steam to turn the turbines.

Turning Uranium into Fuel

Uranium is a metal found in rocks throughout the world and even in seawater. Most uranium is mined in surface, or open-pit, mines. Uranium occurs in several different forms, called isotopes. In each isotope the atom's nucleus contains the same number of protons but a different number of neutrons. The sum of the protons and neutrons equals the isotope's atomic mass. A uranium atom with an atomic mass of 238, for example, has 92 protons and 146 neutrons. This isotope is expressed as U-238 or ^{238}U.

Natural uranium ore is more than 99 percent U-238. Less than 1 percent of natural uranium consists of U-235. However, U-235 is the only natural form of uranium that is fissionable, or easily split apart. It is the only form that can be used to generate nuclear power or make nuclear weapons.

To make uranium ore usable, it is crushed, and uranium oxide is extracted, forming a yellowish powder called yellowcake. Then, through a process called uranium enrichment, the percentage of U-235 is increased. This enriched uranium can be used for various purposes. Most nuclear power plants use low-enriched uranium (LEU). Highly enriched uranium (HEU), or weapons-grade uranium, is used in nuclear weapons. That is why countries with uranium enrichment programs raise alarms about whether they are building nuclear weapons.

After enrichment the uranium is compressed and put inside nonporous ceramic pellets. Each of these little fuel pellets is about the size of a fingertip. The pellets are loaded into long metal rods. Many rods are bundled together inside the reactor core, a steel enclosure where the nuclear fission takes place. The core is enclosed in a containment structure with thick walls made of steel or concrete.

Supply and Demand

As of 2007, eighteen countries were mining uranium ore. Australia holds the world's largest uranium reserves, while Canada is the world's largest uranium exporter. Other uranium-mining countries include Kazakhstan, Russia, Namibia, Niger, and Uzbekistan. While some uranium is mined in the western United States, it is low-grade uranium. The United States imports most of its uranium from Canada, Australia, and other countries.

According to 2008 estimates the world's known uranium reserves are enough to produce nuclear fuel for at least a century. Further, it is believed that almost twice as much uranium is yet to be discovered. New technology could make uranium use more efficient, too, extending the supply much farther into the future.

About 5,500 tonnes of uranium per year are mined from the Ranger mine in Australia.

Many nuclear power plants rely on secondary sources of fuel. That is, they use uranium from nuclear weapons that have been taken out of service. The United States, for example, gets much of its nuclear fuel from Russia, which is converting its disarmed nuclear warheads into fuel. This program, however, is scheduled to end in 2013.

A major problem with the world's uranium supply is that it is not being mined fast enough. In the 1970s and 1980s nuclear power went into decline because of safety and environmental concerns. Many countries stopped investing in uranium processing at that time. As a result, by the early twenty-first century, the supply of enriched uranium for power plants could not keep up with the demand.

Advantages of Nuclear Power

One of the major advantages of nuclear power is that it is a clean resource compared to fossil fuels. Nuclear power plants generate virtually no carbon dioxide or other greenhouse gases. Uranium is also a highly concentrated source of energy. Only a tiny amount generates massive amounts of power.

One fingertip-size uranium fuel pellet produces as much energy as 17,000 cubic feet (480 cubic meters) of natural gas, 1,780 pounds (807 kg) of coal, or 149 gallons (564 L) of oil.

Nuclear power is cheap, too. Although it's expensive to process uranium and build nuclear plants, the cost of electricity generated by nuclear plants is lower than the cost from coal- or gas-fired power plants. The price of nuclear power can also remain stable over time. An increase in the price of uranium has a very small effect on nuclear energy costs compared to increases in coal or gas prices. These factors make nuclear power attractive to less-developed nations.

Nuclear power allows many countries to be energy independent. They don't have to import expensive foreign fuels to produce their electricity. France, for example, relies more heavily on nuclear energy than does any other country in the world. Nuclear power plants generate 78 percent of the country's electricity. When France launched its nuclear power program in the 1970s, a French official explained the decision: "We have no oil, we have no coal, we have no gas, we have no choice."

Disposal of Nuclear Wastes

One major objection to nuclear power is its potential danger to human health and to the environment. Much of that opposition centers around nuclear waste. Waste materials from nuclear power plants emit particles of radiation. Those radioactive particles can reach humans and animals through soil and water, causing cancer, birth defects, and other disorders. So far scientists have found no fail-safe way to treat and dispose of nuclear wastes.

Low-level waste (LLW) consists of items that have come in contact with radiation sources, such as tools and protective clothing used by power plant employees. These materials remain radioactive for only a short time. They are shipped to disposal facilities, where they are buried several feet underground.

The disposal of high-level waste (HLW) is a more serious problem. One type of HLW is spent fuel. After a nuclear reactor has used up the uranium's fuel potential, the leftover U-238

Nuclear Waste: Where to Stash It?

Energy experts worldwide have considered many possibilities for the permanent disposal of nuclear wastes. They include leaving the material in temporary storage sites, burying it under the ocean floor, embedding it in polar ice sheets, sending it into space, burying it deep underground, and burying it on remote, unpopulated islands. Most scientists agree that underground disposal is the best long-term solution.

and other byproducts are known as spent nuclear fuel. Highly radioactive and very dangerous, these wastes are placed in steel or concrete containers and stored above ground near the power plant. As of 2008 the United States had about 121 of these disposal sites in 39 states. However, they are all considered temporary storage sites.

Nuclear Accidents

The danger of accidents is another major objection to nuclear power. The United States has had only one major nuclear accident. It took place at Three Mile Island nuclear power plant near Harrisburg, Pennsylvania, in 1979. Through a combination of human and mechanical errors, the water level in a reactor dropped. That water served as a coolant for the superhot fuel. Without it about half the reactor core melted. This is what is called a partial meltdown. (A meltdown is a total loss of coolant, causing the radioactive fuel to melt through the reactor.)

At Three Mile Island, radioactive gases and contaminated cooling water filled the containment building. Some radioactivity was released into the atmosphere, too, but no one in the plant or in the surrounding community was injured or killed. Nevertheless, the public reaction was extreme. After the accident the United States virtually shut down construction of any new nuclear power plants.

The world's worst nuclear disaster happened in 1986 at Chernobyl, in the former Soviet republic of Ukraine. While workers were conducting a test, they shut off the plant's emergency safety systems. The reactor's core overheated, setting off an explosive, uncontrolled chain reaction. Because the plant lacked an adequate containment structure, tons of radioactive materials were released into the atmosphere over the course of nine days.

After the accident more than 130,000 residents from dozens of villages in the area were evacuated, although some older people refused to leave. The wind spread radioactive dust far beyond the site, causing many health problems in Ukraine, Russia, and Belarus. By 2002, 4,837 children under the age of

The Yucca Mountain Controversy

The U.S. Department of Energy (DOE) hopes to consolidate the nation's radioactive wastes at permanent dump sites. In the 1980s the DOE chose Yucca Mountain, Nevada, as the first of these sites. There the wastes would be enclosed in secure containers and embedded in rock deep underground. Environmental groups, concerned politicians, and local residents have fiercely opposed this plan for years. Among their objections are the potential instability of the rock due to earthquake activity and the danger of transporting wastes cross-country.

eighteen who were living in the area at the time of the accident were diagnosed with thyroid cancer. The incidence of leukemia and other cancers has risen, too, as has the incidence of birth defects in both people and animals.

Nuclear Alternatives

The Chernobyl disaster affected attitudes toward nuclear energy around the world. Many countries decided that nuclear energy was too dangerous to use. If the disaster had an upside, it is that it led to better safety systems and more regulations and oversight being put into place. Meanwhile, scientists developed different, safer reactors with which to produce nuclear power.

A computer-enhanced satellite image was taken April 29, 1986, after the disaster at the Chernobyl power plant. The red sections highlight radioactivity in the surrounding areas of the plant.

One alternative is using nuclear fusion (instead of nuclear fission). In a fusion reaction two or more light-weight atoms are forced together to form a heavier atom. The reaction releases heat energy that can power a steam turbine. This system may not be perfected for many decades. Another alternative is the fast-breeder reactor (FBR). Here, U-238 atoms absorb fast, or high-energy, neutrons to "breed" plutonium-239 (P-239). This isotope is then used as a fuel to produce nuclear power. The breeding process is attractive because it can produce more fuel than it consumes. However, P-239 is also used to make nuclear weapons. While a

few countries use FBRs, the United States and several other countries have stopped their FBR research programs.

An alternative to disposing of spent nuclear fuel is recycling it, or reprocessing it for future use. The recycling process yields various isotopes of uranium, plutonium, and other elements. Several countries currently recycle their spent fuels. In the United States, however, the reprocessing of spent fuel was banned in the late 1970s. This was partly because of concerns about creating plutonium and partly because recycling is more expensive than disposing of old fuel and using fresh uranium.

Scientists continue to search for cleaner, safer, cheaper, and more efficient ways to generate nuclear power. Meanwhile, as the price of fossil fuels continues to increase, many countries are viewing nuclear power as a cheaper alternative to coal-fired power plants. Clearly, they need to pursue their nuclear programs with caution. Nuclear waste and accidents can have a devastating impact on the environment. And nothing has more critical consequences for the global community than a nuclear weapon.

Four
Hydropower: Making a Splash

In the third century CE, the Chinese engineer Ma Jun built a mechanical puppet theater to entertain the emperor. Its wooden figures danced, beat drums, played flutes, waved swords, rode horses, and performed acrobatic stunts. Amazingly, this elaborate device was powered by a wooden waterwheel with a complex system of gears. Though Ma Jun was not the first to use waterwheels, his puppet theater may be history's most unique use of hydropower.

Hydropower is power derived from the force of moving water. That water may be rushing down a river, cascading over a waterfall or dam, or surging forward as ocean waves or tides. Humans have harnessed hydropower since ancient times. They devised ways to capture the kinetic energy of moving water and convert it into mechanical energy. In earlier times that energy was used to perform such tasks as grinding grain. Thanks to hydropower both humans and animals were relieved of tedious physical labor. Today, hydropower is one of the world's leading methods of generating electricity.

From Waterwheels to Hydroelectric Plants

Waterwheels were the earliest machines driven by hydropower. A waterwheel is a large wheel with paddles or buckets around the rim. Erected on a river, the wheel turns as the water flows by, turning the axle in the center of the wheel. The other end of the axle extends inside a watermill, where some mechanical process takes place. In a gristmill, for example, the axle turns a large stone that grinds grain into flour or meal.

The ancient Greeks were using waterwheels to grind grain more than two thousand years ago. By the tenth century CE, engineers had built watermills on rivers throughout the Middle East. By the 1300s watermills in Europe were powering many

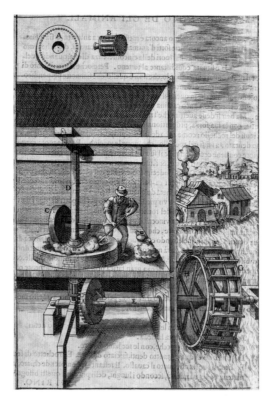

Water is a powerful source of energy. This cutaway diagram illustrates the use of hydropower as it pushes a waterwheel that then turns an axle and large stone to grind meal.

industries. They sawed wood, crushed stone, refined iron ore, polished tools, tanned leather, and processed woolen cloth. When the Industrial Revolution began in the 1700s, giant water-wheels powered textile mills throughout Great Britain. In the northeastern United States, swift-flowing rivers and streams provided power for thousands of textile mills involved in making cotton and woolen cloth.

Meanwhile, scientists were experimenting with electricity and finding ways to put it to practical use. They applied the traditional principle of the waterwheel in a new way. The rushing waters could turn the blades of a turbine, which would power an electric generator. Power lines would carry the electric current to distant locations. This became known as hydroelectric power.

The world's first hydroelectric power plant began operating in 1882 on the Fox River in Appleton, Wisconsin. Thomas Edison had just perfected the electric lightbulb, and the new power plant generated enough electricity to turn on the lights in three buildings. By 1920 hydroelectric plants were providing 25 percent of the nation's electricity.

How Hydroelectric Power Plants Work

A hydroelectric power plant has several basic components. The first is the dam—a wall built across the width of a river. The dam creates a sort of artificial waterfall where water cascades down the face of the dam. The purpose of the dam is to hold back the river's flow, thus increasing the force of the downhill water current. The backed-up water forms a reservoir, or water storage area. Often flooding vast expanses of land, these reservoirs are usually called lakes. Lake Mead, for example, is really a reservoir created by Hoover Dam on the Colorado River. The lake spreads across the Nevada-Arizona border. Like many reservoirs Lake Mead doubles as a recreation area where people enjoy boating and other water sports.

At the base of the dam are huge turbines. Through downward-slanting pipes, water from the reservoir rushes to the turbine, spinning its blades as fast as ninety revolutions per minute. The turbine's shaft spins magnets within

At Hoover Dam in Nevada, millions of gallons of water rush through
pipes toward the dam's generator turbines, producing electricity for
surrounding regions.

wire coils, creating an electric current in the generator. Most hydroelectric plants have several turbines and generators.

Pumped-storage plants use a variation of this process. They have two reservoirs instead of one. Water from the upper reservoir flows through the dam, generating electric power. From there the water enters a lower reservoir instead of continuing downstream. In off-peak hours, when there is less demand for electricity, water from the lower reservoir is pumped back up into the upper reservoir, where it can be used to generate power again.

Downsides of Hydroelectric Power

While hydroelectric power is clean, efficient, renewable, and cheap, it does have some downsides. Because the reservoir submerges a large area of land, habitats are lost and communities must be relocated. This can be a cultural disaster for groups who have lived in the region for hundreds or even thousands of years. Soil particles, or silt, also build up on the reservoir floor behind the dam. Without expensive and time-consuming silt removal, the dam will clog up and stop working. Dams can also burst during earthquakes or torrential rainfalls, causing devastating floods downstream.

The dams affect aquatic life, too. Fish are killed as they get caught in turbines or drop over dams. Reduced water flow in the reservoirs creates warmer water temperatures, eliminating many aquatic species that birds and fish eat. Dams also skim off nutrients, leaving downstream water less healthful. In addition, salmon and some other species return to their place of birth to spawn, or reproduce. This means they have to swim up a dam to reach their spawning grounds. Some salmon manage to ascend dams through a series of powerful leaps, but many do not make it.

Engineers have devised ways to combat some of these problems. Fish migrations are a particular problem in the Pacific Northwest, where large salmon populations migrate downriver to the Pacific Ocean and back upstream to spawn. Fish ladders have been built alongside many dams in this region. Some fish ladders are like rotating elevators that lift fish from the base of the dam up into the reservoir. Other ladders consist

Three Gorges Dam: Destroying the Environment to Save the Environment?

Begun in 1994, China's gigantic Three Gorges Dam is expected to be completed by about 2011. It will raise the level of the Yangtze River, the world's third-longest river, by 575 feet (175 meters). The rising waters will have swallowed up more than 1,200 villages, several major cities, and hundreds of factories, displacing about 1.3 million people. They are being relocated, with government promises of compensation and new homes and jobs.

Environmentalists are concerned about the dam's impact on wildlife. Most of the world's population of critically endangered Siberian cranes spend their winters in wetlands that are being covered by the reservoir. The Yangtze River dolphin, found only in the Yangtze, has become virtually extinct since dam construction began. Hundreds of ancient archaeological sites have been submerged as well, including hanging coffins where ancient people buried their dead in caves high on the cliff sides.

With its rapidly growing population and economy, China faces an ever-increasing demand for electric power. Coal provides most of the country's electricity, and the government expects the Three Gorges Dam to reduce coal consumption by 50 million tons a year.

This fish ladder was constructed at the Bonneville Dam on the Columbia River in Oregon to allow migrating salmon to navigate around the dam.

of a series of pools arranged like stairsteps. The fish can leap upward from pool to pool to reach the reservoir. Fish ladders are not always effective, though, and as a last resort to save a fish species, a dam may be removed. Marmot Dam on Oregon's Sandy River was taken down in 2007 because of its devastating impact on the salmon and steelhead populations.

Damless hydro is an electricity-generating system that eliminates many drawbacks of traditional hydroelectric power plants. Also called run-of-the-river hydro, it uses the kinetic energy of a river's natural flow, not its forced flow over a dam, to generate electricity. One type of damless system diverts fast-flowing water to a turbine in or beside a river. The hydroelectric station at New York's Niagara Falls uses this method. In another system type, turbines or waterwheels are placed in the river, or pipes carry the water downhill, and the flowing water turns the turbines. This system generates much less power than a traditional hydroelectric plant. However, it is less costly to build and maintain, and it is useful for generating power on a small scale in remote regions.

Hydroelectricity Around the World
Worldwide, about 89 percent of all electricity from renewable sources is generated by hydroelectric plants. China is the world leader in hydroelectricity, having produced more than 15 percent of the world's hydroelectric power in 2007. Its Three Gorges Dam on the Yangtze River is the largest hydroelectric power plant in the world. Ranking next in hydropower are Brazil, Canada, and the United States. In some countries hydroelectric plants provide almost all the electric power. For example, 99 percent of Norway's electricity comes from hydroelectric plants.

As of 2008 hydroelectricity accounted for only about 6 percent of U.S. electric power. Among renewable sources in the nation, though, hydroelectricity is the leader. More than two thousand hydroelectric plants are in operation throughout the United States. They generate 75 percent of the country's energy that is generated from renewable resources.

The largest U.S. hydroelectric power plant is Grand Coulee Dam on the Columbia River in Washington State.

Built between 1933 and 1941, it is the fourth-largest hydroelectric plant in the world, generating more than 6,800 MW
of electricity. It took nearly 12 million cubic yards of concrete
to build the dam. With that much concrete, you could build a
sidewalk 4 feet (1.2 m) wide and 4 inches (10 cm) thick and
wrap it twice around the earth at the equator!

Ocean Energy: Tidal and Wave Power

About twice a day the ocean's surface rises and falls, creating
high and low tides. All seacoasts experience two high tides
and two low tides a day. These tidal movements are caused
mostly by the gravitational pull of the moon on the oceans.
The energy of those moving tidewaters can be captured and
converted into electric power with tidal turbines.

Tidal turbines are built in places with fast tidal currents—at
the entrance to a bay, near a rocky point, or between islands.
They can be installed underwater in long rows like the turbines
on wind farms. Another tidal power system is the tidal fence.
It reaches across a narrow channel of water with giant arms
that turn like a turnstile.

Turbines may also be installed in a barrage, or dam, where
gates hold back the tidewaters until they build up enough force
to spin the turbines. The world's first tidal power plant, La
Rance, in Brittany, France, is a tidal barrage. Completed in 1966,
it remained the largest tidal power plant in the world as of 2008.
However, Canada's province of Nova Scotia is planning an even
larger plant offshore, in the Bay of Fundy. Its turbines will be
anchored to the seafloor. In the United States tidal power facilities are being considered in Alaska, California, and Maine.

Tidal power is clean, renewable, and inexpensive. However,
tidal power plants are costly to build and can be used in very
few locations. For a tidal power plant to be effective, the difference between high and low tide must be more than 16 feet
(4.9 m). It is estimated that only about forty sites on Earth
meet this standard. Tidal barrages and tidal fences may also be
harmful to sea life.

The surging energy of ocean waves can be transformed
into electricity, too. Some wave-power systems harness

the energy of waves breaking onshore. Some systems use pumps or turbines to capture wave energy in deep, off-shore waters. Others use a floating structure that bobs up and down on the ocean surface.

Wave energy is being harnessed off the coasts of England, Scotland, Portugal, Canada, Africa, Australia, and other places with powerful wave action. The world's first commercial wave farm, Portugal's Aguçadora Wave Park, was established in 2008. In the United States, researchers are testing various wave-power devices in the waters off the Atlantic and Pacific coasts. They have high hopes for their experiments. Some scientists believe the oceans have the potential to generate more electricity than all the nation's other resources combined.

Five

Solar Power: Capturing the Sunshine

"It was so hot you could fry an egg on the sidewalk." People sometimes say this on a hot summer day. They mean that the Sun is radiating enough energy to evaporate liquids from the egg and change its chemical makeup.

You may not be able to fry eggs this way, but you do benefit from solar energy every day. If you read a book by daylight, you are using solar energy. If you hang out wet laundry on a clothesline, solar energy evaporates the water and dries the clothes. Even when you eat your vegetables, you are taking advantage of solar energy. Your broccoli has converted the Sun's energy into chemical energy, which your body converts to mechanical energy you can use to move.

Solar energy is radiant energy coming from the Sun. That energy arrives on Earth in the form of heat and light. Solar energy is the most abundant of our renewable resources; it is available as long as the Sun keeps shining. In just one hour enough of the Sun's energy reaches the earth to meet the entire world's energy needs for more than a year. The challenge is harnessing that energy and putting it to use.

Solar Thermal Power

Solar energy can be harnessed in many different ways. Some systems convert the Sun's energy into electricity. Others use heat from the Sun to heat water or air directly. These systems are called solar thermal energy (STE) devices, and they capture the Sun's heat with various types of solar thermal collectors.

A greenhouse is a simple type of solar thermal device. Its glass roof and walls let the Sun's heat in and trap it inside. The air becomes so warm that the plants inside it grow fast. Some solar cookers work like greenhouses. They trap heat under a glass or plastic cover, cooking the food inside. Other solar cookers use a mirror or a sheet of metal to reflect sunlight and heat onto the food.

Many homes use solar hot-water heaters. This type of heater's thermal collector is a large, flat metal box mounted on the roof with water pipes running through it. The Sun heats the water, which runs into a storage tank. The hot water can then be used for taking showers, washing clothes, and so on.

By capturing the Sun's energy, this rooftop solar heater is a cost effective way to heat water for a single home.

In some systems, pipes with hot water run under the floor to heat the home. Solar water heaters can also be used to heat the water in swimming pools, car washes, and Laundromats.

Photovoltaic Solar Power

The most common way of generating electricity from sunlight is with solar photovoltaics (PV). The word *photovoltaics* is built from two words. *Photo* comes from the Greek word for light, and *volt* relates to electricity. The volt is named after the Italian physicist Alessandro Volta (1745–1827). Solar cells are the devices used to generate PV power. Usually made of silicon, they are also known as photovoltaic cells or photoelectric cells. They convert sunlight directly into electricity.

Sunlight travels in bundles of energy called photons. When sunlight shines on a solar cell, the silicon absorbs some of the photons' energy. The absorbed energy excites the silicon atoms' electrons, knocking some of them loose. Those freed-up electrons create an electrical current. This is called the photovoltaic effect. The electricity is then drawn off by metal wires and used. Solar cells can power small objects, such as calculators and wristwatches. They can be integrated into a building's structure to provide power for the building. They also can generate great amounts of electricity for a whole region. Solar cells are even used to power communications satellites.

One solar cell is all it takes to power a calculator. However, most uses of solar power require a lot of solar cells. Solar panels, or photovoltaic modules, are groups of interconnected solar cells mounted within a frame. Several modules are linked together to form a solar array, or photovoltaic array. Some homes and businesses have a rooftop solar array. Photovoltaic power stations, or PV power plants, may have thousands of solar arrays to supply electricity to a broad geographical area. Most have tracking devices that allow the solar panels to follow the Sun's path across the sky.

Concentrating Solar Power

As a child you may have used a magnifying glass to focus a hot spot of sunlight on the sidewalk. If you did, you were

This solar power station near Toledo, Spain, has thousands of solar arrays that supply electricity to the surrounding region.

concentrating solar energy into one small point. Concentrating solar power (CSP) systems do the same thing. They are also called concentrating systems or concentrating solar thermal systems.

Like photovoltaic systems, CSP systems convert sunlight into electricity. Using mirrors or some other reflective material, they focus sunlight onto one spot. This increases the sunlight's energy many times, creating intense heat. That heat eventually drives a generator that produces electricity. CSP devices include solar dish/engine systems, parabolic trough systems, and power towers.

Solar dish/engine systems have large, round dishes that look like satellite dishes. They collect the Sun's heat and focus it onto a receiver. The receiver transfers the heat into a fluid or a gas within an engine. As the heated substance expands, it drives a turbine that powers an electric generator. As of 2008 no dish/engine systems were ready for large-scale commercial use. However, they are being tested at facilities such as New Mexico's Sandia National Laboratories.

Parabolic trough systems use long, rectangular troughs of curved mirrors to collect sunlight. The mirrors focus the sunlight onto pipes that run down the center of the trough. Oil inside the pipes heats up, and that heat is used to boil

Parabolic mirrors at the Nevada Solar One power plant concentrate heat on pipes that contain oil, heating it to more than 700 degrees Fahrenheit.

water into steam that powers an electric generator. The Nevada Solar One power plant near Boulder City, Nevada, uses this system. Opened in 2007, it uses 760 troughs with more than 180,000 mirrors.

Power towers, or solar towers, work in many different ways. In one system a tall tower is surrounded by hundreds of mirrors called heliostats. The mirrors swivel to follow the Sun's path, concentrating sunlight on a receiver at the top of the tower. Air, oil, or liquid salt in the receiver heats water to produce steam that drives a turbine.

The massive PS10 tower in Seville, Spain, is the first of many power towers the country hopes to build. Other power towers generate electricity in South Africa and in Israel's Negev Desert. Plans are also under way to build power towers in Africa's Sahara desert.

Weighing the Merits

Solar power's biggest advantage is its abundance: the Sun provides more energy than humans will ever need. Solar power is clean, too. It produces no wastes or pollution. Solar power systems are versatile as well. They can be placed on rooftops, in

The Odeillo Solar Furnace

One type of concentrating solar power device is the solar furnace. The world's largest solar furnace is in Odeillo, France. Its sixty-three moving mirrors collect sunlight and direct it into a huge curved reflector. The reflector focuses a beam onto a spot on top of a tower, where temperatures can reach over 5,432 °F (3,000 °C).

Payback Time

How long do you have to use a solar cell before it generates as much energy as it took to produce it? That figure is called the energy payback time (EPBT). Standard silicon-based solar cells have an EPBT of 2.2 to 2.7 years, while thin-film solar cells have an EPBT of 1.7 years.

backyards, on mountaintops, or in deserts. Solar power is also a good way to generate electricity in remote areas where it's difficult to run power lines.

An obvious disadvantage of solar power is that the Sun does not shine at night, so solar energy can be collected only in the daytime. Clouds and dust in the atmosphere also cut down on the solar radiation that reaches the ground. This makes a power storage system or a backup power source necessary. Solar power plants and solar panels are also expensive to build. However, once built, they are inexpensive to operate. Compared to other types of power plants, they do not need much maintenance.

Worldwide Usage and Outlook

Germany is the world leader in solar power use. It generated 47 percent of the world's solar PV power in 2007. Spain came in second, at 23 percent, followed by Japan (8 percent) and the United States (7.8 percent). Solar power has an enthusiastic following in the United States. Nevertheless, among all U.S. energy resources, it generates the least electricity.

Solar power is growing fast, though. From 2006 to 2007 worldwide use of solar PV power grew 62 percent. Almost every year brings another "world's largest" solar PV plant. Australia, Portugal, Germany, and Spain were all building huge-capacity plants in 2008. The largest PV power station in the United States is Nellis Solar Power Plant in Nevada, with 70,000 solar panels.

The demand for silicon for solar cells is so high that the supply cannot keep up. This has led to the development of alternatives such as thin-film photovoltaics. Thin films are made of very thin layers of light-sensitive materials. They are easier and cheaper to make than silicon-based solar cells, and they can be integrated into roof shingles, siding, and windows. Thin films accounted for 12 percent of the world's solar PV energy production in 2007. As global demand for solar power keeps rising and researchers develop ever more efficient power-generation systems, the future of solar energy is sunny.

Six
Wind Power: Harnessing the Breezes

Stand on the seashore, and you're likely to feel a strong breeze. Sea breezes are created when the air above dry land heats up more quickly than the air over water. As the warm air over the land rises up, the cooler air above the ocean rushes in to take its place. That rush of air is the breeze you feel.

To put it simply, wind is moving air. Winds blow because the Sun heats the atmosphere and the earth's surface unevenly throughout the day and the year. Wherever a sun-warmed pocket of air rises, cool air surges into the void, creating a wind.

There are many kinds of winds, from the large wind belts that circle the earth to the little puffs of air you feel when you take a walk. Many conditions generate wind and affect where and how it blows. Some of these factors are the earth's rotation, local climate patterns, plant cover, and such geographic features as mountains and bodies of water.

How Wind Power Works

Throughout the ages people have found ways to harness the wind's energy. They have used wind to sail ships, grind grain, lift water, saw wood, charge batteries, and generate electricity. In all these activities the wind's kinetic energy is transformed into another form of energy to do some kind of work.

Wind turbines are machines that capture the wind's energy and convert it into mechanical energy. They have blades, or propellers, that turn as the wind blows. Wind turbines are built on tall towers so their blades can capture wind currents high above the ground. The blades are mounted on a central shaft. As the wind blows the blades round and round, the shaft spins. That spinning motion either does some kind of mechanical work or powers a generator that produces electricity.

Windmills are a simple type of wind turbine that people have used for more than a thousand years. Today, many residents of rural areas use small wind turbines to generate the electricity they need. Large, modern wind turbines

Wind turbines generate energy by capturing the energy of wind with their spinning blades and convert that energy into electric power.

The Pickens Plan

The billionaire oilman T. Boone Pickens is an out-spoken advocate for wind power. He points out that the Great Plains states have the greatest wind energy potential in the world. To take advantage of this resource, Pickens plans to build what would be the world's largest wind farm, stretching from Pampa, Texas, northward across the Great Plains. According to his Pickens Plan, announced in 2008, wind energy can replace natural gas in power plants, and that natural gas could be used to fuel vehicles.

operate on wind farms to produce the quantity of electricity needed by homes and businesses.

A wind farm may consist of only a couple of wind turbines or as many as several hundred. Ideally, it is located in a place that has a constant, year-round wind flow. Shorelines, mountainous areas, and wide-open plains are common sites for wind farms. As of 2008 the world's largest wind farm was the Horse Hollow Wind Energy Center, near Sweetwater, Texas. Its 421 wind turbines spread across almost 47,000 acres (19,000 hectares).

Some wind farms are located in offshore waters to take advantage of the strong winds there. Typically, an offshore wind tower is mounted on a monopile foundation—a metal cylinder driven deep into the seafloor. In 2008 one of the world's largest offshore wind farms was Denmark's 80-turbine Horns Rev, located several miles offshore in the North Sea. At the time both Great Britain and Texas were planning even larger offshore facilities.

The History of Wind Power

People have used wind energy since prehistoric times. In farming cultures people used the wind for winnowing grain. This separates the edible grain from the chaff, or outer husk. They would throw the mixture into the air. Then the wind carried off the lighter chaff, while the heavier grains fell to the ground. In some parts of the world people still winnow grain this way.

Winds have filled the sails of boats for thousands of years. As early as 3000 BCE, ancient Egyptians affixed cloth sails to their boats so they could travel swiftly along the Nile River. By the 1500s wind-powered ships outfitted with dozens of sails were voyaging around the world.

The earliest windmills appeared in the 600s in ancient Persia (now Iran). They were vertical-axis windmills: that is, their blades were mounted on a vertical shaft. At the bottom of the shaft was a grindstone. As the wind turned the blades, the shaft rotated, and the grindstone ground the grain. Europeans were using windmills to grind grain by the 1100s. They used horizontal-axis windmills that stood upright, like the ones we know today. Europeans also devised the

postmill—a windmill mounted on a tall post so it can swivel around as the wind direction changes.

In the 1400s the Dutch began using windmills to drain land. Much of their country, today's Netherlands, lies below sea level, and the danger of flooding is constant. They used windmills to pump water off the lowlands so they could farm them.

A Scottish professor, James Blyth, built the first windmill that generated electricity in 1887. Wind power caught on in the United States after small farm turbines were introduced in the 1920s. By the 1930s thousands of rural farms across the country received their electricity from backyard windmills. Wind power declined after the 1936 Rural Electrification Act. This measure extended electric power lines to rural areas from coal- or gas-fueled power plants and hydroelectric plants.

Wind Power Worldwide

In the late twentieth century, wind power began to make a comeback worldwide. At first the cost of building large wind turbines and wind farms was very high. The costs are dropping, though, as wind turbines get larger and more efficient, wind technology improves, and governments and private companies invest more money in wind power. Today's wind turbines are gigantic, standing up to 410 feet (125 m) tall, with blades stretching 148 feet (45 m)—and plans are under way for even larger ones.

By the end of 2007, seventy-four countries were using wind energy, supplying 1.3 percent of the world's electricity. Germany generated the most wind-powered electricity, followed by the United States. Next in line were Spain, India, China, Denmark, Italy, and France. Denmark was using wind power to meet around 20 percent of its electricity needs.

In the United States, Texas leads all the other states in wind power production. Next are California, Minnesota, Iowa, Washington State, and Colorado. Wind produced only slightly more than 1 percent of U.S. electricity in 2008. But wind power is showing a spectacular growth rate. From 1998 to 2008, U.S. wind power generation increased more than 1100 percent, or eleven times. Between 2005 and 2008 it more than doubled. Many experts estimate that, at its

Wind turbines are tremendous in size. Compare the size of this technician to that of the blades.

full potential, wind can supply more than 20 percent of the nation's electric power.

Practical Considerations

Wind power offers many advantages. For example, it is a renewable energy source, and the supply is endless. As long as the Sun keeps shining, the wind will keep blowing. While fuel prices may go up and down, making the price of fuel-generated electricity fluctuate, the price of wind-powered electricity will remain stable, because no fuel is purchased. Wind power is also environmentally friendly. Wind turbines emit no carbon dioxide or other greenhouse gases. Although wind farms cover a lot of land area, that land is still available for other uses. Farmers can safely graze cattle or raise crops on a wind farm.

Wind farms do have drawbacks. Some people complain that wind turbines are unsightly and ruin their view of nature. This is of great concern in areas that depend on tourism to bring money into the economy. Another obvious downside of

Wind Farms: A Great Future Ahead?

U.S. wind farms generated about 48 billion kilowatt hours (kWh) of electricity in 2008. That's enough to power about 4.5 million homes. If a traditional coal- or gas-fired power plant produced that much electricity, it would release more than 28 million tons of carbon dioxide into the atmosphere every year. It would take more than 17,000 square miles (44,030 sq km) of forest to absorb that much carbon dioxide. The U.S. Department of Energy (DOE) is exploring the possibility of generating 20 percent of U.S. electricity from wind by the year 2030. The DOE estimates that this would reduce carbon dioxide emissions from electricity production by 825 million metric tons.

wind power is that the wind does not always blow. This means that other resources will always be needed to supply backup power. To address this problem, many large wind installations are integrated with a community's other electricity sources on the power grid. As one source's energy supply dips, another source kicks in. This is an ideal way to make the most of such a valuable resource.

Seven

Biomass: New Life for an Old Fuel

Huddle in the glow of a fireplace on a chilly winter's night or roast marshmallows and hot dogs around a campfire. Like your prehistoric ancestors, you are enjoying the benefits of burning wood as a fuel.

For thousands of years wood was the main fuel used by humans. People developed the skill to start fires by making sparks with stones or by using the friction of wood against wood. With wood-burning fires they could cook food and survive in cold climates. Only in the mid–1800s did coal begin to replace wood as a fuel. In some parts of the world wood is still the main fuel used for cooking and generating warmth.

Biomass as an Energy Resource

In terms of energy resources, wood is a form of biomass. Biomass is any organic material—that is, any material derived from plants or animals. Besides wood, biomass includes crops, farm wastes, plant oils, animal fats, and even some kinds of garbage. When biomass is used as a fuel, its chemical energy is converted into heat, electricity, or mechanical energy.

Transportation fuels made from biomass are called biofuels. They are mostly made from crops. Some researchers consider biofuels to be one of the best alternatives to fossil fuels, while others underscore the practical limitations of using them. The most widely used biofuels are ethanol and biodiesel.

Ethanol as a Fuel

Ethanol is also known as ethyl alcohol or grain alcohol. It is made from the sugars and starches found in plants such as corn and sugarcane. About 70 percent of the gasoline sold in the United States contains some amount of ethanol. This ethanol-gasoline blend is called gasohol. The amount of ethanol is designated by an E number. For example, E10 gasohol contains 10 percent ethanol, and E85 gasohol contains 85 percent ethanol. Most U.S. gasoline that contains ethanol is E10 gasohol, and most U.S. cars can run on E10. However, flexible-fuel or flex-fuel vehicles (FFVs) can run on gasohol with ethanol levels as high as E85.

The United States makes almost all of its ethanol from corn. The corn is converted into ethanol through either the wet-milling or dry-milling process. Wet milling was common in the ethanol industry's early days. This process turns out a variety of corn products. Today, dry-milling plants dedicated to producing ethanol are more common. They grind the grain into flour and add water to make a starchy mash. Enzymes are added to convert the starch to sugar. Then yeast is added to ferment the sugar, converting it to ethanol. Finally, the ethanol is distilled to remove impurities.

From 2004 to 2007 U.S. corn-ethanol production almost doubled, from 3.4 billion gallons (12.9 billion L) in 2004 to 6.5 billion gallons (24.5 billion L) in 2007. That made the United States the world's largest producer of ethanol.

Brazil: An Ethanol Giant

Brazil is the world leader in using ethanol as a transportation fuel. The country was the world's second-largest ethanol producer in 2007, with an output of 5 billion gallons (18.9 billion liters). Ethanol is so widely used in Brazil because the

government requires all vehicles to use an ethanol-gasoline blend or even pure ethanol as a fuel.

Brazil makes most of its ethanol from bagasse—the stalks and other plant material left over after processing sugarcane into sugar. The bagasse is crushed, and the sugary cane juice that comes out is made into ethanol. Producing ethanol this way is

Ethanol (in beaker) is a product of corn. In 2008, 9 billion gallons of ethanol were produced in the United States.

inexpensive. It uses a waste product instead of a food crop, and bagasse does not have to be converted into sugar, as corn does.

Ethanol Feasibility Issues

Because ethanol is made from plant material, it is a much cleaner burning fuel than gasoline. According to 2007 estimates, ethanol use reduced U.S. greenhouse gas emissions by about 10.1 million tons. Ethanol is also biodegradable, breaking down quickly in soil or water.

Critics of corn-based ethanol, however, point out that it takes a lot of "dirty" energy to produce it. The corn must be planted, fertilized, harvested, trucked to the ethanol plant, and processed. Most of the vehicles and machinery that do these things run on fossil fuels. Also, corn raised for ethanol is heavily dosed with nitrogen fertilizers. The nitrous oxide released from the fertilizer is much more damaging to the environment than carbon dioxide.

Corn-based ethanol raises questions about food supplies, too. Corn is a valuable food crop for both people and animals. Some form of corn is an ingredient in thousands of food products on grocery store shelves. Corn is also a major U.S. export. By 2008, however, about 34 percent of the U.S. corn crop was being used for ethanol. With less corn available as food, the price of corn and many other foods could rise.

A promising alternative to corn-based ethanol is cellulosic ethanol. It is made from wood, grasses, and the inedible parts of food crops. Enzymes are used to break down the cellulose, or plant fiber, into sugars, which are then fermented by bacteria into ethanol. In the early twenty-first century the United States had only a few cellulosic ethanol plants. They make ethanol from wood, wood chips, wheat straw, corncobs, and orange peels. Researchers are working on ways to make cornstalks, switchgrass, poplar trees, and other plant materials into ethanol, too.

Biodiesel as a Fuel

Biodiesel is a fuel made from vegetable oils and animal fats. It is a renewable alternative to diesel fuel, which is made from petroleum. Most tractors, buses, and large trucks have engines

Table 1. Ethanol Source Crops and Energy Yield

Source crop	Gallons of ethanol per year from 1 acre of crop	Net energy yield (units of energy generated for every 1 unit of energy spent to make the fuel)
Corn	354	1.5
Sugarcane	662	8+
Sugar beets	714	1.9
Switchgrass	1,150	4

Source: Lester R. Brown, *Plan B 2.0: Rescuing a Planet Under Stress and a Civilization in Trouble* (NY: W.W. Norton & Co., 2006), pp. 34–35.

that require diesel fuel. They can use fuel containing biodiesel instead, without any changes to their engines. Biodiesel can be used full strength or blended with regular diesel fuel. As with gasohol, the blends are numbered according to how much biodiesel they contain. For example, B20 is 20 percent biodiesel, and B75 is 75 percent biodiesel. An engine may have to be modified to work with B100, or pure biodiesel.

Most biodiesel in the United States is made with soybean oil, while some is made with leftover grease and cooking oils from restaurants and factories. Oils are converted into biodiesel through a process called transesterification. It involves adding an alcohol to the oil to induce a chemical reaction. The resulting products are biodiesel and a small amount of an oily liquid called glycerin.

Waste vegetable oil (WVO) is a growing source of biodiesel. It can be collected from fast-food restaurants, snack-food factories, or potato-processing plants that use huge deep-fryers. According to 2000 estimates, the United States produces more than 3 billion gallons (11 billion L) of WVO a year. Ordinarily, these oils are discarded. WVO is filtered to remove impurities, heated, and then converted to biodiesel. Some people even do this in their garages or backyard sheds.

These teens filter waste vegetable oil from their local restaurants to be converted to biodiesel and used by several school buses in their district.

From Chickens to Jets

Tyson Foods is the largest meat-processing company in the world. It processes about 25 percent of the country's meat supply, including chicken, pork, and beef. After trimming all that meat, tons of scrap fat are left over. Tyson's operations produce about 2.3 billion pounds (1 billion kg) of animal fat every year. The company plans to convert much of that fat into biodiesel. Tyson's Dynamic Fuels plant, in Geismar, Louisiana, scheduled to open in 2010, is expected to produce 75 million gallons (284 million L) of synthetic fuels a year. Much of that fuel will go to Louisiana's Barksdale Air Force Base for its B-52 bombers. The B-52 is the first Air Force jet approved to use synthetic fuels.

Some countries use other kinds of oils to make biodiesel. They use rapeseed (canola) oil, sunflower oil, palm oil, peanut oil, or coconut oil. Animal fats used to produce biodiesel include tallow from beef, lard from pork, and chicken fat.

Biopower

Using biomass to generate heat and electricity is called biopower. Next to hydropower, biomass accounts for more electricity than any other renewable energy resource in the United States.

Wood is the most widely used form of biomass. It generates more than two-thirds of the country's biopower. Most of this wood is waste material from timber and paper mills. It includes bark, wood chips, sawdust, and scrap wood. Many wood and paper mills burn their own wastes to provide power for their plants. Some other industries and city power plants also burn wood wastes to generate electricity.

The other major source of biopower is municipal solid waste (MSW), better known as city garbage. Americans produced more than 251 million tons of MSW in 2006. That amounts to about 4.6 pounds (2 kg) of waste per person every day. Some of that waste can be recycled, such as paper, metal, glass, plastic, and grass clippings. Today, more than 32 percent of MSW in the United States is recycled.

Unfortunately, not all recyclable material gets recycled. It is sent to landfills, along with other MSW, such as food scraps and discarded furniture and clothing. However, dozens of facilities, called waste-to-energy plants, are converting that garbage into electric power. They burn the MSW, producing heat that turns water into steam. The steam drives turbines that power electric generators. In 2006, 12.5 percent of the country's MSW was converted to electricity this way.

There are other ways to generate energy from wastes. As biomass rots, it releases methane gas—also called landfill gas or biogas. Some landfills have systems for collecting that gas and using it as a fuel to generate electricity. Some farmers also shovel their farm animals' manure into a tank called a digester, which produces methane gas. They may use the gas to provide electricity for their farms or sell the electricity to their local power companies.

The Outlook for Biomass

The major advantage of biomass is that it is a renewable energy source. We can always plant more crops and trees. Another advantage is that biomass stores its energy until it is needed, so it is available at any time, unlike solar or wind power.

Biomass can provide electricity for farms, remote villages, industries, or even small cities. However, burning biomass presents some environmental problems. Burning biomass releases carbon dioxide into the atmosphere, and burning MSW releases toxic materials that can seep into the soil and water supply. In the mid–1990s the Environmental Protection

Methane gas is collected from wells at this Michigan landfill and then used to generate electricity.

Agency (EPA) began issuing rulings about pollution-control measures that waste-to-energy plants must adopt.

As for biofuels, they offer the hope of reducing the nation's dependence on imported oil. Using biofuels drastically reduces the amount of greenhouse gases released into the atmosphere by fossil fuels. However, more research and government support are needed to find cleaner, more efficient ways to produce biofuels in the future.

Eight

Geothermal Power:
Heat from the Earth

More than 10,000 years ago the Paleo-Indians of North America discovered hot-water springs. While bathing in these springs, they found the waters' heat and minerals had remarkable healing properties. They believed such springs were dwelling places of the Great Spirit, who brought forth the healing powers of Mother Earth. Hot springs became zones of peace, where warring groups laid aside their weapons and refreshed themselves in the waters together.

Hot springs are just one example of the earth's vast geothermal resources. The word *geothermal* comes from two Greek words: *geo* (earth) and *therme* (heat). Geothermal energy is the heat energy stored deep within the planet. It has a tremendous potential for producing electric power. Heat trapped within the earth contains 50,000 times as much energy as all the oil and natural gas resources in the entire world. The challenge is to harness that energy to meet human needs.

Where Does Geothermal Energy Come From?
Geothermal energy originates in the earth's core, or center, 4,000 miles (6,440 km) beneath the surface. Temperatures there can

reach 7,000 °F (3,870 °C) or more. Surrounding the core is the mantle. Its top layer is composed of molten rock called magma, which can reach more than 1,000 °F (540 °C). Earth's crust, several miles thick, sits atop this magma. The deeper we drill into the planet, the hotter it gets. Every 328 feet (100 m) below ground we go, the temperature increases about 5.4 °F (3 °C).

When underground water comes near the magma, the water boils or turns into steam. This underground pocket of moisture is called a geothermal reservoir. When the moisture reaches a crack in the earth's crust, it bursts through the crack. If it emerges as hot water, it creates a hot-water spring. If it comes out in the form of steam and other gases, it creates a fumarole. Where hot water, steam, and gases emerge together, the eruption is called a geyser. *(Geyser* comes from the Icelandic word *geysir,* meaning "gusher.") Old Faithful is a famous geyser in Yellowstone National Park in Wyoming. It spews water and gas high into the air, faithfully, about once every 74 minutes. However, eruption intervals can vary between 45 and 110 minutes.

Geothermal energy is an important resource in areas with active volcanoes. Molten rock is very close to the surface there. One such area is the so-called Ring of Fire—the lands surrounding the Pacific Ocean. In the United States that includes many of the western states. The island nation of Iceland is volcanically active, too. Much of its heat and electricity come from geothermal sources.

Geothermal Power Worldwide

Geothermal energy is a growing resource worldwide. As of 2005, twenty-four countries were using geothermal power to generate electricity, and twenty-two more countries were planning geothermal projects.

Iceland is considered the star of geothermal energy production. It uses geothermal sources for heating homes as well as generating electricity. The country is fully powered by renewable resources, with geothermal energy meeting 17 percent of its electricity and 87 percent of its heating

Geothermal energy is stored beneath the earth's surface. Yellowstone
National Park's Old Faithful geyser is a good example of the power
available from geothermal energy.

needs. The Philippines also has an aggressive geothermal program. Geothermal energy generates 27 percent of the islands' electricity. Other countries using geothermal power include Australia, Japan, New Zealand, and the United States.

The United States produces about 35 percent of the world's geothermal electricity, making it the world leader in geothermal power production. Geothermal power provides less than 1 percent of U.S. electricity needs. Still, it is the nation's fourth-largest renewable energy source, after hydroelectric, biomass, and wind power. By 2008, seven states were generating geothermal power—Alaska, California, Hawaii, Nevada, New Mexico, Utah, and Idaho. California alone produces more geothermal power than any country.

Geothermal Power Plants

Geothermal power plants capture the earth's heat energy and convert it to electric power. They use one of three methods—the dry steam, flash steam, and binary systems. In the dry steam system, hot water comes to the earth's surface in the form of steam. That steam is used to drive an electric turbine. The dry-steam field at The Geysers in California is the world's largest geothermal power complex. Located north of San Francisco, this group of twenty-two power plants generates about 725 MW of electricity. They provide electricity for much of northern California.

The flash-steam system uses very hot water, hotter than 360 °F (182 °C). It is vaporized, or "flashed," into steam, and the steam drives a turbine. The binary system uses lower-temperature water, which is more readily available than superhot water or steam. In this system the water temperature may be as low as 100 to 300 °F (38 to 149 °C). This is not hot enough to flash into steam. However, that water is used to heat another liquid with a lower boiling point, such as ammonia or isobutane. This secondary liquid flashes into steam, which then drives a turbine.

Scientists are also experimenting with enhanced geothermal systems (EGS), sometimes called heat mining. This is a way to capture heat from hot, dry rocks. To reach hot rock,

Discharged salt, algae, and silica-rich water from the Svartsengi
Geothermal Power Plant in Iceland formed the famed Blue Lagoon.

a hole is drilled deep into the earth, much like those drilled for oil. Then water is pumped down the hole, and the hot rocks heat the water. The hot water is brought back to the surface and flashed into steam to power a turbine.

Geothermal Heat Pumps and Direct Use

If you've ever explored an underground cave, you probably felt a bit chilly down there. That is because, just a few feet below the earth's surface, the ground keeps a constant temperature of about 50 to 60 °F (10 to 16 °C). That temperature remains the same through sweltering summers and frigid winters. Because of the constant temperature, geothermal energy can be drawn from shallow ground to both heat and cool entire buildings.

With a geothermal heat pump (GHP) system, a liquid such as water circulates in underground pipes, transferring heat to or from the ground. This brings warmer air into a building during the winter. In the summer the system cools a building by removing warm air and transferring it into the ground. Another type of GHP system, the open-loop system, uses water from a well, pond, or lake near the building in the heat-transfer process. GHP systems can be used anywhere in the United States, and hundreds of thousands of homes, schools, and commercial buildings are currently using them.

Another way to use geothermal resources near the earth's surface is direct use. It involves piping underground hot water directly to the place that needs heat. Many facilities in the United States use this system. Hot water heats office build-ings, homes, and greenhouses. It heats the water on fish farms, processes milk in dairy plants, and dehydrates, or dries, veg-etables. In some communities with cold winters a network of hot-water pipes runs underground to melt the ice and snow on roads and sidewalks.

Practical Issues

Geothermal power offers many advantages. First, it is renew-able. The planet's core is expected to keep generating heat for a few billion more years. Geothermal energy is clean, too. Because geothermal power plants do not burn fuel,

they produce virtually no air pollution. Small quantities of pollutants are sometimes released, but in infinitely smaller amounts than from coal plants equipped with emissions-control devices.

Geothermal energy is available for twenty-four hours every day, unlike wind and solar energy. In addition, geothermal power stations do not take up much space, so they make little impact on the environment. The Geysers area in California, for example, is teeming with wildlife and remains an attractive hunting ground.

One drawback to geothermal energy is that there are not many geographical locations where a geothermal power station can be built. It is also expensive to explore and drill for suitable sites. Once a power station is built, though, the cost of producing electricity is very low. Meanwhile, on a smaller scale, direct-use and heat-pump systems are available for homes and businesses built in most areas.

Geothermal technology is improving all the time, especially with the increasing demand for clean, renewable energy. Over time the obstacles and costs will continue to decline as geothermal energy contributes more to our energy needs.

An Ancient Resource Goes Modern

For thousands of years people have used geothermal energy for cooking, heating, and bathing. The ancient Romans built buildings around hot springs to create public bathhouses. People went there to relax and soak in the hot mineral waters. The Romans built an elaborate bathhouse complex in the English city of Bath, which was once part of the Roman Empire. For the ancient Greeks hot springs were healing centers. Ancient Chinese and Egyptian peoples made use of hot springs, too.

Converting geothermal energy into electricity began in the early twentieth century. The world's first geothermal power plant was built at Larderello, Italy, in 1904. The second was not built until 1958, at Wairakei, New Zealand. Both plants are still in operation. California's The Geysers, built in 1960, was the first U.S. geothermal power plant. Other geothermal plants now operate in countries around the world.

Nine
Managing Energy for a Cleaner Planet

By almost all accounts we are in the midst of an energy crisis. Human energy needs are skyrocketing. At the beginning of the twenty-first century the world's population was consuming about 15 terawatts (TW) of power every year. (A terawatt is 1 trillion watts.) By 2050 world consumption is expected to double, reaching 30 TW a year.

Clearly, we face daunting challenges in the way we manage and consume energy. We must conserve energy, use it more efficiently, and make the most of clean, renewable resources. Some of these challenges call for measures people can take on their own. They require personal responsibility, individual decision making, and changes in familiar habits and lifestyles. Other challenges can be met only by governments working in partnership with citizens and private industries.

Clean Air, Fuel Efficiency, and Oil Independence

Over the years the U.S. government has enacted many laws and regulations to reduce the emission of greenhouse gases. Congress passed the first Clean Air Act in 1963, with major revisions in 1970, 1990, and other years. It is one of many laws

It is important to find alternate sources of energy as U.S. gas consumption and prices increase.

setting limits on the amount of greenhouse gases a vehicle or power plant can emit.

Corporate Average Fuel Economy (CAFE) standards were introduced in 1975. CAFE standards tell U.S. automakers how fuel efficient their vehicles must be. The idea is that if cars can

run farther on each gallon of gasoline, Americans will consume less gas. As of 2008 those standards were 27.5 miles per gallon (11.7 km per liter) for regular passenger cars and 22.5 miles per gallon (9.6 km per liter) for sports utility vehicles (SUVs), vans, and pickup trucks. These standards will continue to be raised.

Besides environmental concerns, there is the issue of energy independence. In 2008 the United States spent about $440 billion on imported oil—more than four times its expenditure in 2002. How can we free ourselves of dependence on foreign oil? Should we try to extract the oil we need from U.S. land?

At the end of 2006 the proven oil reserves in the United States amounted to almost 21 billion barrels. That sounds like a lot of oil, but because Americans consume oil at the rate of 21 million barrels a day, it would take less than three years to use that up. This option also overlooks the issue of greenhouse gas emissions. Considering air quality and climate-change issues, we need to be moving away from fossil fuels, not figuring out how to find more.

Why Not Just Switch to Alternative Fuels?

Making the switch to alternative fuels is dependent on many factors. Consumers must demand hybrid or alternative-fuel vehicles. They must be willing to buy these vehicles even if they are more expensive and less convenient to maintain than standard vehicles. Automakers must be willing to invest billions of dollars in new technologies. Oil companies must accept declining gasoline sales. And the government must encourage and support the research and development of alternative fuels and cars.

Meanwhile, for alternative vehicles to be practical on a large scale, we need an infrastructure to support them. For example, there would have to be a nationwide network of stations where people could fill up on hydrogen or recharge their electric batteries. This, too, calls for more money and commitment.

Energy Efficiency at Home

Your own home is another place to tackle energy issues. In many states residents can choose an electric plan that

Turn It Off! Unplug It! Take a Walk!

There are many simple ways to cut down on your energy consumption. For example, put your computer on sleep mode when you're not using it. It consumes less energy that way. When you finish charging your cell phone, unplug the charger. It keeps using electricity as long as it's plugged in. Don't keep the TV on just to provide background noise, and turn off the lights when you leave a room. Instead of taking a car everywhere, try walking, riding your bike, or taking public transportation once in a while. You'll see the world from a different perspective, get some exercise, and cut down on greenhouse-gas emissions.

generates some of its power with renewable sources. There is also a variety of ways to make a home more energy efficient. Insulation can reduce the need for heating and air conditioning. Adding weather stripping around windows cuts down on heating needs, too.

For home lighting, fluorescent lightbulbs are a good choice because they consume less energy than incandescent bulbs. Compact fluorescent lightbulbs (CFLs) can be 75 percent more energy efficient than regular bulbs. Light-emitting diode (LED) lightbulbs are highly efficient, too. LED lighting is used in many streetlights, traffic lights, and lighted signs.

When people buy such appliances as refrigerators, washing machines, and TVs, they can look for the EnergyGuide label. It states how much electricity the appliance uses, compared with other models. It also states about how much it will cost to use the appliance for a year. Better still, many appliances also carry an Energy Star label. These appliances consume an average of 20 to 30 percent less energy than similar products.

Why Not Just Switch to Renewable Electricity Sources?

Private companies cannot develop renewable energy industries by themselves. One of the biggest factors in these industries' growth is the financial support of the U.S. government. Companies that invest in wind, solar, geothermal, and other forms of renewable energy have received a production tax credit (PTC) since the 1990s. The PTC is a powerful incentive for investing in the development of renewable energy industries. It makes the difference between building alternative energy facilities and not building them. However, the PTC expires every year or two and must be reapproved by Congress and the president. In years when the credit lapses, renewable energy developments decline dramatically.

What Can *You* Do?

Much of the decision making about energy resources rests in the hands of adults. But there are plenty of hands-on ways you can conserve energy and reduce greenhouse-gas emissions

EnergyGuide labels inform consumers how much energy that device uses per year and how it compares to other models.

yourself (see sidebar on p. 93). These may seem like small, insignificant measures, but they add up. Remember—without thinking about it, you are burning up more than 5 tons of coal every year. You may not be able to save the whole planet by yourself, but you can do your part.

You can do even more by learning all you can about energy issues and talking with others about them. Speak up, start a dialogue, and have fact-based arguments to offer. Listen to politicians, energy company executives, and scientists and weigh what they say against what you've learned. You yourself may be in their shoes someday, and now is a good time to begin forming your policies.

The worldwide outlook for energy resources is uncertain. Undoubtedly, the use of alternative energy is expanding fast. Manufacturers, for example, cannot make wind turbines and solar cells fast enough to keep up with the demand. Still, as the world's population grows and developing countries expand their industries, the consumption of such fossil fuels as coal and oil will continue to rise.

Environmentally active citizens and green-technology companies can do only so much. The global environment will be at risk unless governments around the world adopt long-term national policies in favor of renewable energy resources. Only then can we look forward to a cleaner, greener planet for generations to come.

Notes

Chapter One

p. 7, "Every day about 29 pounds...": U.S. Department of the Interior, Bureau of Land Management. "Coal and Electricity Equivalents, 2001." http://www.blm.gov/ut/st/en/prog/energy/coal/electricity_conversion.html (accessed 28 August 2008).

p. 7, "...500 gallons (1,892 liters) of gasoline.": U.S. Department of Energy, Energy Information Administration. "Energy Efficiency," http://www.eia.doe.gov/kids/energyfacts/saving/efficiency/savingenergy.html (accessed 28 August 2008).

p. 16, "...13 to 24 million BTUs per ton...": Union of Concerned Scientists. "Clean Energy: How Coal Works," http://www.ucsusa.org/clean_energy/fossil_fuels/offmen-how-coal-works.html (accessed 28 August 2008).

p. 16, "...2,000 kilowatt hours of electricity.": "Coal and Electricity Equivalents."

p. 16, "...5,000 BTUs of power...": Micropyretics Heaters International. "Watt Calculator," http://www.mhi-inc.com/Converter/watt_calculator.htm (accessed 28 August 2008).

p. 17, "By about 1885, coal had replaced…": U.S. Department of Energy, Energy Information Administration, "History of Energy in the United States, 1635–2000," http://www. eia.doe.gov/emeu/aer/eh/frame.html (accessed 26 August 2008).

p. 17, "…consumption of petroleum and natural gas quadrupled.": "History of Energy in the United States."

Chapter Two

p. 20, "That includes almost two-thirds…": U. S. Department of Energy, "Fossil Fuels," http://www.doe.gov/energysources/ fossilfuels.htm (accessed 12 August 2008).

p. 21, "About 84 percent of greenhouse gases…": U.S. Department of Energy, Energy Information Administration, "Emissions of Greenhouse Gases in the United States 2006," 28 November 2007, p. 1, http://www. eia.doe.gov/oiaf/1605/ggrpt/carbon.html (accessed 12 August 2008).

p. 23, "The United States emitted about 7.8 billion tons…": "Emissions of Greenhouse Gases," p. 5.

p. 23, "In 2006, 44 percent of U.S. greenhouse gas emissions…": U.S. Department of Energy, Energy Information Administration, "What are greenhouse gases and how much are emitted by the United States?" http://tonto.eia.doe.gov/energy_in_brief/greenhouse_ gas.cfm (accessed 12 August 2008).

p. 25, "Saudi Arabia is the world's largest…": U.S. Department of Energy, Energy Information Administration, "2006 World Oil Production," http://tonto.eia.doe.gov/country/ index.cfm?view = production (accessed 26 August 2008).

p. 25, "Americans use almost 21 million barrels of oil…": U.S. Department of Energy, Energy Information

Administration, "Petroleum Basic Statistics," http://www.eia.doe.gov/basics/quickoil.html (accessed 6 September 2008).

p. 25, "The next-largest consumers…": U.S. Department of Energy, Energy Information Administration, "2006 World Oil Consumption," http://tonto.eia.doe.gov/country/index.cfm?view=consumption (accessed 26 August 2008).

p. 25, "…imports more than 10 million barrels…": "Petroleum Basic Statistics."

p. 25, "Canada is the largest supplier…": U.S. Department of Energy, Energy Information Administration, "U.S. Imports by Country of Origin," http://tonto.eia.doe.gov/dnav/pet/pet_move_impcus_a2_nus_epc0_im0_mbblpd_a.htm (accessed 26 August 2008).

p. 25, "…more oil than it produces.": BP, *Statistical Review of World Energy 2008*, June 2008, pp. 8, 11. http://www.bp.com/productlanding.do?categoryId=6929&contentId=7044622 (accessed 9 August 2008).

p. 28, "In 2006, 20 percent of U.S. greenhouse gas emissions…": "What are greenhouse gases?"

p. 28, "Coal production began 300 to 400 million years ago…": U.S. Department of Energy, "How Fossil Fuels Were Formed," http://fossil.energy.gov/education/energylessons/coal/gen_howformed.html (accessed 14 August 2008).

p. 30, "…coal produces about half…": U.S. Department of Energy, "Coal: Our Most Abundant Fuel," http://fossil.energy.gov/education/energylessons/coal/gen_coal.html (accessed 14 August 2008).

p. 30, "In 2006, 36 percent of U.S. greenhouse gas emissions…": "What are greenhouse gases?"

Chapter Three

p. 35, "As of 2008, nuclear power provided...": "Net Generation by Energy Source: Total (All Sectors)."

p. 35, "The United States has . . . Russia.": World Nuclear Association, "World Nuclear Power Reactors 2007–08 and Uranium Requirements," 8 August 2008, http://www.world-nuclear.org/info/reactors.html (accessed 30 August 2008).

p. 37, "As of 2007, eighteen countries...": World Nuclear Association. "World Uranium Mining," July 2008, http://www.world-nuclear.org/info/inf23.html (accessed 14 November 2008).

p. 37, "Australia holds the world's largest...": World Nuclear Association, "Australia's Uranium and Nuclear Power Prospects, September 2008, http://www.world-nuclear.org/info/inf48.html (accessed 22 September 2008).

p. 37, "...Canada is the world's largest...": MiningWatch Canada, "Uranium," http://www.miningwatch.ca/index.php?/Uranium (accessed 22 September 2008).

p. 37, "Other uranium mining countries...": "World Uranium Mining."

p. 37, "The United States imports most of its uranium...": Massachusetts Institute of Technology, "Lack of fuel may limit U.S. nuclear power expansion," *Tech Talk*, 4 April 2007, p. 6, http://web.mit.edu/newsoffice/2007/techtalk51-22.pdf (accessed 12 July 2008).

p. 37, "...for at least a century.": Nuclear Energy Agency, "Uranium resources sufficient to meet projected nuclear energy requirements long into the future," press communiqué, 3 June 2008, http://www.nea.fr/html/general/press/2008/2008-02.html (accessed 30 August 2008).

p. 38, "…scheduled to end in 2013.": "Lack of fuel may limit U.S. nuclear power expansion."

p. 38, "…could not keep up with the demand.": "Lack of fuel may limit U.S. nuclear power expansion."

p. 39, "One fingertip-size uranium fuel pellet…": Nuclear Energy Institute, "How It Works: Nuclear Power Plant Fuel." http://www.nei.org/howitworks/ nuclearpowerplantfuel/ (accessed 15 July 2008).

p. 39, "Although it's expensive . . . coal or gas prices.": International Energy Agency, *IEA Energy Technology Essentials: Nuclear Power*, No. 4, March 2007, pages 2–3, http://www.iea.org/textbase/techno/essentials4.pdf (accessed 15 July 2008).

p. 39, "…78 percent of the country's electricity.": World Nuclear Association, "Nuclear Power in France," May 2008, http://www.world-nuclear.org/info/inf40.html (accessed 15 July 2008).

p. 39, "We have no oil…": Ryan, Margaret. "Nuclear renaissance faces realities." *Platts Insight: 2005 Global Energy Outlook,* pp. 20–21, December 2004, http:// www.platts.com/Magazines/Insight/december/index. html (accessed 15 July 2008).

p. 41, "…121 of these disposal sites…": Office of Civilian Radioactive Waste Management, "What are spent nuclear fuel and high-level radioactive waste?" July 2007, http://www.ocrwm.doe.gov/factsheets/ doeymp0338.shtml (accessed 30 August 2008).

p. 41, "…4,837 children…": World Health Organization, "Health Effects of the Chernobyl Accident and Special Health Care Programmes," 2006, p. 23, http://www. who.int/ionizing_radiation/chernobyl/who_chernobyl_ report_2006.pdf, (accessed 14 November 2008).

Chapter Four

p. 51, "It will raise the level of the Yangtze... 1.3 million people";
"...reduce coal consumption by 50 million tons a year.":
Wertz, Richard R. *Special Report: Three Gorges Dam*,
http://www.ibiblio.org/chinesehistory/contents/07spe/
specrep01.html (accessed 10 August 2008).

p. 53, "Worldwide, about 89 percent...": Observatoire
des énergies renouvelables, "Worldwide electricity
production from renewable energy sources." *Stats
and Figures Series*, Edition 2007, http://www.energies-
renouvelables.org/observer/html/inventaire/Eng/
conclusion.asp (accessed 11 August 2008).

p. 53, "China is the world leader...": *Statistical Review of World
Energy 2008*, p. 38.

p. 53, "Ranking next in hydropower...": *Statistical Review of
World Energy 2008*, p. 38.

p. 53, "...99 percent of Norway's electricity...": Statistics
Norway, "Electricity Statistics, 2006, Table 1: Main figures,
1989–2006." http://www.ssb.no/elektrisitetaar_en/tab-
2008-05-30-01-en.html (accessed 8 August 2008).

p. 53, "...6 percent of U.S. electric power.": "Net Generation
by Energy Source: Total (All Sectors)."

p. 53, "They generate 75 percent...": U.S. Department of
Energy, Energy Information Administration, "Electricity
Net Generation from Renewable Energy by Energy Use
Sector and Energy Source, 2002–2006," April 2008,
http://www.eia.doe.gov/cneaf/solar.renewables/page/
rea_data/table1.11.html (accessed 28 August 2008).

p. 53, "The largest U.S. hydroelectric power plant . . . equator!":
U.S. Department of Energy Bureau of Reclamation,
"Grand Coulee Dam Statistics and Facts," November 2007,

http://www.usbr.gov/pn/grandcoulee/pubs/factsheet.
pdf (accessed 11 August 2008).

p. 54, "...forty sites on Earth...": U.S. Department of Energy,
"Ocean Tidal Power," http://www.eere.energy.gov/
consumer/renewable_energy/ocean/index.cfm/
mytopic = 50008 (accessed 11 August 2008).

Chapter Five

p. 56, "In just one hour...": U.S. Department of Energy, Solar
Energy Technology Programs, "Light and the PV Cell,"
http://www1.eere.energy.gov/solar/pv_cell_light.html
(accessed 21 July 2008).

p. 60, "...it uses 760 troughs...": ACCIONA Energy,
"ACCIONA's Nevada Solar One—Demonstrating the
Commercial Competitiveness of Solar Energy," http://
www.nevadasolarone.net/the-plant (accessed 22 July
2008).

p. 62, "Standard silicon-based solar cells...": U.S. Department
of Energy, Energy Information Administration,
"Photovoltaics Basics," http://www1.eere.energy.gov/
solar/pv_basics.html (accessed 24 July 2008).

p. 62, "Germany is the world leader . . . (7.8 percent).": "2007
World PV Industry Report Highlights," *Marketbuzz,* 17
March 2008, http://www.solarbuzz.com/Marketbuzz
2008-intro.htm (accessed 22 September 2008).

p. 63, "...it generates the least electricity.": U.S. Department
of Energy, Energy Information Administration, "Net
Generation by Other Renewables: Total (All Sectors),"
Electric Power Monthly, 28 October 2008, http://www.
eia.doe.gov/cneaf/electricity/epm/table1_1_a.html
(accessed 15 November 2008).

p. 63, "...solar PV power grew 62 percent.": "2007 World PV
Industry Report Highlights."

p. 63, "Thin films accounted for 12 percent...": "2007 World PV Industry Report Highlights."

Chapter Six

p. 68, "...seventy-four countries . . . France.": World Wind Energy Association, "Wind turbines generate more than 1% of the global electricity," press release, 21 February 2008, http://www.wwindea.org/home/images/stories/pr_statistics2007_210208_red.pdf (accessed 24 July 2008).

p. 68, "...around 20 percent of its electricity needs.": Risoe DTU, "Wind Energy: A Visionary Match," http://risoe-staged.risoe.dk/Reasearch/sustainable-energy/wind-energy.aspx (accessed 15 November 2008).

p. 68, "...Texas leads all the other states...": American Wind Energy Association, "Wind Power Outlook 2008," p. 2, http://www.awea.org/pubs/documents/Outlook_2008.pdf (accessed 25 July 2008).

p. 68, "...slightly more than 1 percent...": American Wind Energy Association, "Installed U.S. Wind Power Capacity surged 45% in 2007," press release, 17 January 2008, http://www.awea.org/newsroom/releases/AWEA_Market_Release_Q4_011708.html (accessed 25 July 2008).

p. 68, "...increased more than 1100 percent...doubled.": "Net Generation by Other Renewables: Total (All Sectors)."

p. 68, "...20 percent of the nation's electric power.": "Wind Power Outlook 2008," p. 3.

p. 70, "U.S. wind farms...28 million tons...": "Installed U.S. Wind Power Capacity."

p. 70, "...17,000 square miles...": American Wind Energy Association, "Wind Energy Fast Facts," http://www.

awea.org/newsroom/pdf/Fast_Facts.pdf (accessed 30 August 2008).

p. 70, "...825 million metric tons.": U.S. Department of Energy, "20% Wind Energy by 2030: Increasing Wind Energy's Contribution to U.S. Electricity Supply," May 2008, www.20percentwind.org/20percent_Wind_Flyer. pdf (accessed 22 September 2008).

Chapter Seven

p. 72, "People developed...wood against wood.": *Encyclopaedia Britannica Online*, "Fire (combustion)," http://www. britannica.com/EBchecked/topic/207750/fire (accessed 28 July 2008).

p. 73, "About 70 percent of the gasoline...": American Coalition for Ethanol, "Ethanol 101," http://www. ethanol.org/index.php?id=34&parentid=8 (accessed 28 July 2008).

p. 73, "...U.S. corn ethanol production almost doubled...": Runge, C. Ford, and Benjamin Senauer. "How Ethanol Fuels the Food Crisis," *Foreign Affairs*, 28 May 2008, http://www.foreignaffairs.org/20080528faupdate 87376/c-ford-runge-benjamin-senauer/how-ethanol-fuels-the-food-crisis.html (accessed 28 July 2008).

p. 73, "Brazil... 5 billion gallons...": Renewable Fuels Association, "Industry Statistics: Ethanol," http://www. ethanolrfa.org/industry/statistics/ (accessed 26 July 2008).

p. 75, "According to 2007 estimates, ethanol use reduced...": Renewable Fuels Association, "Ethanol Facts: Environment," http://www.ethanolrfa.org/resource/ facts/ environment/ (accessed 27 July 2008).

p. 75, "The nitrous oxide...": "How Ethanol Fuels the Food Crisis."

p. 75, "...about 34 percent of the U.S. corn crop...": CattleNetwork, "Percentage of Corn Crop Used for Ethanol," http://www.cattlenetwork.com/Content.asp? ContentID=230813 (accessed 28 July 2008).

p. 77, "...United States produces more than 3 billion gallons...": Alternative Fuel Companies, "Vegetable Oil Fuel," http:// www.alternativefuelcompanies.com/vegetable-oil-fuel (accessed 26 July 2008).

p. 78, "From Chickens to Jets": Ehrlich, David, "Tyson, Syntroleum to build biodiesel plant in Louisiana," Cleantech Group, 13 November 2007, http://media. cleantech.com/2076/tyson-syntroleum-to-build-biodiesel-plant (accessed 23 September 2008).

p. 78, "Next to hydropower, biomass accounts for more...": "Electricity Net Generation from Renewable Energy."

p. 78, "It generates more than two-thirds...": "Net Generation by Energy Source: Total (All Sectors)."

p. 79, "Americans produced...every day.": U.S. Environmental Protection Agency, "Municipal Solid Waste Generation, Recycling, and Disposal in the United States: Facts and Figures for 2006," November 2007, http://www.epa. gov/garbage/pubs/msw06.pdf (accessed 28 July 2008).

p. 79, "Today, more than 32 percent...": "Municipal Solid Waste Generation, Recycling, and Disposal."

p. 79, "In 2006, 12.5 percent of the country's MSW...": "Municipal Solid Waste Generation, Recycling, and Disposal."

Chapter Eight

p. 82, "More than 10,000 years ago... waters together.": Lund, John W., "Historical Impacts of Geothermal Resources on the People of North America." *Geo-Heat Center Quarterly Bulletin,* vol. 16, no. 4 (October 1995), p. 10, http://geoheat.oit.edu/bulletin/bull16-4/art2.pdf (accessed 4 August 2008).

p. 82, "...50,000 times as much energy...": U.S. Department of Energy, "Geothermal Energy," http://www.eere. energy.gov/states/alternatives/geothermal.cfm (accessed 8 September 2008).

p. 83, "Every 328 feet...": California Energy Commission, "Geothermal Energy," *Energy Story,* http://www. energyquest.ca.gov/story/chapter11.html (accessed 5 August 2008).

p. 83, "If it emerges as hot water . . . *geysir,* meaning 'gusher.'": Alyssa Kagel, Diana Bates, and Karl Gawell, *A Guide to Geothermal Energy and the Environment,* Geothermal Energy Association, April 2007, http://www.geo-energy. org/publications/reports/Environmental%20Guide. pdf, p. 56 (accessed 6 August 2008).

p. 83, "As of 2005, twenty-four countries...": Gawell, Karl, and Griffin Greenberg, "Update on World Geothermal Development, 2007 Interim Report," *Geothermal Energy Association,* 1 May 2007, p. 1. http://www.geo-energy. org/publications/reports/GEA World Update 2007.pdf (Accessed 6 August 2008).

p. 83, "The country is fully powered...": "Update on World Geothermal Development," p. 6.

p. 85, "Geothermal energy generates 27 percent...": "Guide to Geothermal Energy," p. 4.

p. 85, "The United States produces about 35 percent...": National Renewable Energy Laboratory, Geothermal Technologies Program, "About Geothermal Electricity," http://www. nrel.gov/geothermal/ (accessed 4 August 2008).

p. 85, "...the nation's fourth-largest renewable...": "Net Generation by Other Renewables: Total (All Sectors)."

p. 85, "By 2008, seven states were generating geothermal power...": Slack, Kara, "U.S. Geothermal Power Production and Development Update," Geothermal Energy Association, 7 August 2008, http://www.geo-energy.org/publications/reports/Geothermal_Update_August_7_2008_FINAL.pdf, p. 2, (accessed 10 September 2008).

p. 85, "The dry-steam field at The Geysers . . . northern California.": Calpine Corporation, "Welcome to The Geysers," http://www.geysers.com (accessed 4 August 2008).

p. 87, "GHP systems can be used anywhere...": "Update on World Geothermal Development," p. 17.

Chapter Nine

p. 90, "By 2050 world consumption...": "The power and the glory," in "Special Report: The Future of Energy," *Economist*, 19 June 2008, http://www.economist.co.uk/specialreports/displayStory.cfm?story_id = 11565685 (accessed 10 September 2008).

p. 92, "...spent about $440 billion on imported oil...": Reuters, "US Oil Import Bill to Top $400 Billion this Year, Says Petroleum Intelligence Weekly," press release, 7 March 2008, http://www.reuters.com/article/pressRelease/idUS236508+07-Mar-2008+BW20080307 (accessed 10 September 2008).

p. 92, "...almost 21 billion barrels.": *Petroleum Basic Statistics.*

Further Information

Books

Cartlidge, Cherese. *Alternative Energy.* Yankton, SD: Erickson Press, 2008.

Craddock, David. *Renewable Energy Made Easy: Free Energy from Solar, Wind, Hydropower, and Other Alternative Energy Sources.* Ocala, FL: Atlantic Publishing Group, 2008.

De La Garza, Amanda (editor). *Biomass: Energy from Plants And Animals.* Detroit, MI: Greenhaven Press, 2006.

Gibilisco, Stan. *Alternative Energy Demystified.* New York: McGraw-Hill Professional, 2007.

Hall, Linley Erin (editor). *Critical Perspectives on Energy and Power.* New York: Rosen Publishing Group, 2006.

Hunnicutt, Susan C. (editor). *Foreign Oil Dependence.* Detroit, MI: Greenhaven Press, 2008.

Ingram, W. Scott. *The Chernobyl Nuclear Disaster*. New York: Facts on File, 2005.

Morgan, Sally. *The Pros and Cons of Coal, Gas, and Oil*. New York: Rosen Central, 2008.

Scientific American Magazine, Editors of. *Oil and the Future of Energy*. Guilford, CT: Lyons Press, 2007.

Sherman, Jill. *Oil and Energy Alternatives*. Edina, MN: Abdo Publishing Company, 2009.

Websites

Energy Kid's Page (Energy Information Administration, Department of Energy)
www.eia.doe.gov/kids/
This site contains a wealth of energy facts as well as energy-related activities and games.

Energy Sources: Renewables
www.energy.gov/energysources/renewables.htm
This site includes descriptions of each renewable resource used in the United States, with links to the latest Department of Energy statistics and research programs.

Energy Story
www.energyquest.ca.gov/story/index.html
This energy education website from the California Energy Commission discusses electricity, fossil fuels, renewable resources, and energy conservation.

Renewable Energy Basics (National Renewable Energy Laboratory)
www.nrel.gov/learning/re_basics.html
This site contains in-depth but clear explanations of solar, wind, biomass, hydrogen, geothermal, ocean, and hydropower energy resources.

Students' Corner (U.S. Nuclear Regulatory Commission)
www.nrc.gov/reading-rm/basic-ref/students.html
Explains nuclear energy, nuclear reactors, radiation, and radioactive wastes.

Bibliography

ACCIONA Energy. "ACCIONA's Nevada Solar One— Demonstrating the Commercial Competitiveness of Solar Energy." http://www.nevadasolarone.net/the-plant (accessed 22 July 2008).

Alternative Fuel Companies. "Vegetable Oil Fuel." http://www. alternativefuelcompanies.com/vegetable-oil-fuel (accessed 26 July 2008).

American Coalition for Ethanol. "Ethanol 101." http://www. ethanol.org/index.php?id=34&parentid=8 (accessed 28 July 2008).

American Wind Energy Association. "Installed U.S. Wind Power Capacity surged 45% in 2007." Press release, 17 January 2008. http://www.awea.org/newsroom/releases/AWEA_ Market_Release_Q4_011708.html (accessed 25 July 2008).

———. "Wind Energy Fast Facts." http://www.awea.org/ newsroom/pdf/Fast_Facts.pdf (accessed 30 August 2008).

———. "Wind Power Outlook 2008." http://www.awea.org/ pubs/documents/Outlook_2008.pdf (accessed 25 July 2008).

BP. "Statistical Review of World Energy 2008." June 2008. http://www.bp.com/productlanding.do?categoryId=6929&contentId=7044622 (accessed 9 August 2008).

Brown, Lester R. *Plan B 2.0: Rescuing a Planet Under Stress and a Civilization in Trouble.* NY: W.W. Norton & Co., 2006.

Bullis, Kevin. "Cellulosic Ethanol Plant Opens." Massachusetts Institute of Technology, *Technology Review*, 28 May 2008. http://www.technologyreview.com/Energy/20828/ (accessed 26 July 2008).

California Energy Commission. "Geothermal Energy," in *Energy Story.* http://www.energyquest.ca.gov/story/chapter11.html (accessed 5 August 2008).

Calpine Corporation. "Welcome to The Geysers." http://www.geysers.com (accessed 4 August 2008).

CattleNetwork. "Percentage of Corn Crop Used for Ethanol." http://www.cattlenetwork.com/Content.asp?ContentID=230813 (accessed 28 July 2008).

Central Intelligence Agency. "Rank Order, Electricity Consumption." *CIA World Factbook.* https://www.cia.gov/library/publications/the-world-factbook/rankorder/2042rank.html (accessed 24 July 2008).

Economist. "The power and the glory," in "Special Report: The Future of Energy," 19 June 2008. http://www.economist.co.uk/specialreports/displayStory.cfm?story_id=11565685 (accessed 10 September 2008).

Ehrlich, David. "Tyson, Syntroleum to build biodiesel plant in Louisiana." Cleantech Group, 13 November 2007. http://media.cleantech.com/2076/tyson-syntroleum-to-build-biodiesel-plant (accessed 23 September 2008).

Encyclopaedia Britannica Online. "Fire (combustion)." http://www.britannica.com/EBchecked/topic/207750/fire (accessed 28 July 2008).

Environmental Defense Fund. "Geothermal Energy: Power from the Earth." http://www.edf.org/page.cfm?tagID=22830 (accessed 4 August 2008).

Gabbard, Alex. "Coal Combustion: Nuclear Resource or Danger." *ORNL (Oak Ridge National Laboratory) Review,* vol. 26, no. 34, 1993, rev. 5 February 2008. http://www.ornl.gov/info/ornlreview/rev26034/text/colmain.html (accessed 28 August 2008).

Gawell, Karl, and Griffin Greenberg. "Update on World Geothermal Development, 2007 Interim Report." Geothermal Energy Association, May 1, 2007. http://www.geo-energy.org/publications/reports/Environmental%20Guide.pdf, page 56 (accessed 6 August 2008).

International Atomic Energy Agency. "Nuclear Power Plant Information."http://www.iaea.org/cgi-bin/db.page.pl/pris.charts.htm (accessed 9 July 2008).

International Energy Agency. "IEA Energy Technology Essentials: Nuclear Power." No. 4, March 2007. http://www.iea.org/textbase/techno/essentials4.pdf, pages 2–3 (accessed 15 July 2008).

———. "Key World Energy Statistics 2007." http://www.iea.org/Textbase/nppdf/free/2007/key_stats_2007.pdf (accessed 6 August 2008).

———. "Trends in Photovoltaic Applications: Survey report of selected IEA countries between 1992 and 2006." http://www.iea-pvps.org/products/download/rep1_16.pdf (accessed 22 July 2008).

Kagel, Alyssa, Diana Bates, and Karl Gawell. *A Guide to Geothermal Energy and the Environment.* Geothermal Energy Association, April 2007. http://www.geo-energy.org/publications/reports/Environmental%20Guide.pdf, page 56 (accessed 6 August 2008).

Lund, John W. "Historical Impacts of Geothermal Resources on the People of North America." *Geo-Heat Center Quarterly Bulletin,* vol. 16, no. 4 (October 1995). http://geoheat.oit.edu/bulletin/bull16-4/art2.pdf (accessed 4 August 2008).

Marketbuzz. "2007 World PV Industry Report Highlights," 17 March 2008. http://www.solarbuzz.com/Marketbuzz2008-intro.htm (accessed 22 September 2008).

Massachusetts Institute of Technology. "Lack of fuel may limit U.S. nuclear power expansion." *Tech Talk,* 4 April 2007. http://web.mit.edu/newsoffice/2007/techtalk51-22.pdf (accessed 12 July 2008).

Micropyretics Heaters International. "Watt Calculator." http://www.mhi-inc.com/Converter/watt_calculator.htm (accessed 28 August 2008).

MiningWatch Canada: "Uranium." http://www.miningwatch.ca/index.php?/Uranium (accessed 22 September 2008).

National Renewable Energy Laboratory. Geothermal Technologies Program. "About Geothermal Electricity." http://www.nrel.gov/geothermal/geoelectricity.html (accessed 4 August 2008).

Nelson, Jenny. *The Physics of Solar Cells: Photons In, Electrons Out.* London: Imperial College Press, 2003.

Nuclear Energy Agency. "Uranium resources sufficient to meet projected nuclear energy requirements long into the future." Press communiqué, 3 June 2008. http://www.nea.fr/html/general/press/2008/2008-02.html (accessed 30 August 2008).

Nuclear Energy Institute. "How It Works: Nuclear Power Plant Fuel." http://www.nei.org/howitworks/nuclearpowerplantfuel/ (accessed 15 July 2008).

Observatoire des énergies renouvelables. "Worldwide electricity production from renewable energy sources," *Stats and Figures Series*, Edition 2007. http://www.energies-renouvelables. org/observ-er/html/inventaire/Eng/conclusion.asp (accessed 11 August 2008).

Renewable Fuels Association. *Ethanol Facts: Environment.* http://www.ethanolrfa.org/resource/facts/environment/ (accessed 27 July 2008).

———. "Industry Statistics: Ethanol." http://www.ethanolrfa. org/industry/statistics/ (accessed 26 July 2008).

Reuters. "US Oil Import Bill to Top $400 Billion this Year, Says Petroleum Intelligence Weekly." Press release, 7 March 2008. http://www.reuters.com/article/pressRelease/ idUS236508+07-Mar-2008+BW20080307 (accessed 10 September 2008).

Risoe DTU. "Wind Energy: A Visionary Match." http://risoe-staged.risoe.dk/Research/sustainable-energy/wind-energy. aspx (accessed 15 November 2008).

Runge, C. Ford, and Benjamin Senauer. "How Ethanol Fuels the Food Crisis." *Foreign Affairs*, 28 May 2008. http://www. foreignaffairs.org/20080528faupdate87376/c-ford-runge-benjamin-senauer/how-ethanol-fuels-the-food-crisis.html (accessed 28 July 2008).

Ryan, Margaret. "Nuclear renaissance faces realities." *Platts Insight: 2005 Global Energy Outlook,* December 2004. http:// www.platts.com/Magazines/Insight/december/index.html, pages 20–21 (accessed 15 July 2008).

Slack, Kara. "U.S. Geothermal Power Production and Development Update." Geothermal Energy Association, 7 August 2008. http://www.geo-energy.org/publications/reports/Geothermal_Update_August_7_2008_FINAL.pdf, page 2 (accessed 10 September 2008).

Statistics Norway. "Electricity Statistics, 2006. Table 1: Main figures, 1989–2006." http://www.ssb.no/elektrisitetaar_en/tab-2008-05-30-01-en.html (accessed 8 August 2008).

Union of Concerned Scientists. "Clean Energy: How Coal Works." http://www.ucsusa.org/clean_energy/fossil_fuels/offmen-how-coal-works.html (accessed 28 August 2008).

United Nations Statistics Division. "Environment Statistics." *Environment Glossary.* http://unstats.un.org/unsd/environmentgl/ (accessed 27 August 2008).

U.S. Department of Energy. "Coal: Our Most Abundant Fuel." http://fossil.energy.gov/education/energylessons/coal/gen_coal.html (accessed 14 August 2008).

———. "Fossil Fuels." http://www.doe.gov/energysources/fossilfuels.htm (accessed 12 August 2008).

———. "Geothermal Energy." http://www.eere.energy.gov/states/alternatives/geothermal.cfm (accessed 8 September 2008).

———. "A History of Geothermal Energy in the United States." http://www1.eere.energy.gov/geothermalhistory.html (accessed 4 August 2008).

———. "How Fossil Fuels Were Formed." http://fossil.energy.gov/education/energylessons/coal/gen_howformed.html (accessed 14 August 2008).

———. "Learning About Fossil Fuels." http://fossil.energy.
gov/education/energylessons/index.html (accessed 14 August
2008).

———."OceanTidalPower."www.eere.energy.gov/consumer/
renewable_energy/ocean/index.cfm/mytopic=50008
(accessed 11 August 2008).

———. "20% Wind Energy by 2030: Increasing Wind Energy's Contribution to U.S. Electricity Supply." May 2008.
http://www.20percentwind.org/20percent_Wind_Flyer.pdf
(accessed 22 September 2008).

U.S. Department of Energy. Energy Information Administration. "Annual Energy Review 2007: Electricity Net Generation:
Total (All Sectors), 1949–2007." http://www.eia.doe.gov/aer/
txt/ptb0802a.html (accessed 28 August 2008).

———. "Coal Demand." October 2008. http://www.eia.doe.
gov/neic/infosheets.coaldemand.html (accessed 14 November
2008).

———. *Electric Power Monthly.* "Net Generation by Energy
Source: Electric Utilities, 1994 through April 2008." 25 August
2008. http://www.eia.doe.gov/cneaf/electricity/epm/table1_2.
html (accessed 8 September 2008).

———. "Electricity Net Generation from Renewable
Energy by Energy Use Sector and Energy Source, 2002–
2006." April 2008. http://www.eia.doe.gov/cneaf/solar.
renewables/page/rea_data/table1.11.html (accessed 28
August 2008).

———. "Emissions of Greenhouse Gases in the United
States 2006." 28 November 2007. http://www.eia.doe.
gov/oiaf/1605/ggrpt/carbon.html (accessed 12 August
2008).

————. "Energy Efficiency." http://www.eia.doe.gov/kids/ energyfacts/saving/efficiency/savingenergy.html (accessed 28 August 2008).

————. "Energy Kid's Page: Nuclear Energy." http://www.eia. doe.gov/kids/energyfats/sources/non-renewable/nuclear.html (accessed 14 July 2008).

————. "Historical Renewable Energy Consumption by Sector and Energy Source, 2000–2006." April 2008. http://www.eia. doe.gov/cneaf/solar.renewables/page/rea_data/table1.5b.html (accessed 28 August 2008).

————. "History of Energy in the United States, 1635–2000." http://www.eia.doe.gov/emeu/aer/eh/frame.html (accessed 26 August 2008).

————. "Net Generation by Energy Source: Total (All Sectors)." 28 October 2008. http://www.eia.doe.gov/ cneaf/electricity/epm/table1_1.html (accessed 14 November 2008).

————. "Net Generation by Other Renewables: Total (All Sectors)," 28 October 2008. http://www.eia.doe.gov/cneaf/ electricity/epm/table1_1_a.html (accessed 15 November 2008).

————. "Petroleum Basic Statistics." http://www.eia.doe.gov/ basics/quickoil.html (accessed 6 September 2008).

————. "2006 World Oil Consumption." http://tonto.eia. doe.gov/country/index.cfm?view=consumption (accessed 26 August 2008).

————. "2006 World Oil Production." http://tonto.eia.doe.gov/ country/index.cfm?view=production (accessed 26 August 2008).

———. "U.S. Imports by Country of Origin." http://tonto.
eia.doe.gov/dnav/pet/pet_move_impcus_a2_nus_epc0_im0_
mbblpd_a.htm (accessed 26 August 2008).

———. "What are greenhouse gases and how much are emitted by the United States?" http://tonto.eia.doe.gov/energy_in_
brief/greenhouse_gas.cfm (accessed 12 August 2008).

———. "World Net Electricity Generation by Type, 2005." 17
September 2007. http://www.eia.doe.gov/emeu/international/
RecentElectricityGenerationByType.xls (accessed 26 August
2008).

———. "World Net Nuclear Electric Power Generation, Most
Recent Annual Estimates, 1980–2007." 20 June 2008 http://
www.eia.doe.gov/emeu/international/RecentNuclearGenera-
tionKilowatthours.xls (accessed 26 August 2008).

———. "World Total Net Electricity Generation, Most Recent
Annual Estimates, 1980–2006." 13 September 2007. http://
www.eia.doe.gov/emeu/international/RecentTotalElectric-
Generation.xls (accessed 9 July 2008).

U.S. Department of Energy. Office of Civilian Radioactive
Waste Management. "What are spent nuclear fuel and high-
level radioactive waste?" July 2007. http://www.ocrwm.
doe.gov/factsheets/doeymp0338.shtml (accessed 30 August
2008).

U.S. Department of Energy. Office of Nuclear Energy. "The
History of Nuclear Energy." DOE/NE-0088. http://local.
ans.org/mi/Teacher_CD/Historical Info/DOE-NE-0088.pdf
(accessed 12 July 2008).

U.S. Department of Energy. Solar Energy Technology
Programs. "Light and the PV Cell." http://www1.eere.
energy.gov/solar/pv_cell_light.html (accessed 21 July 2008).

———. "Photovoltaics Basics." http://www1.eere.energy.gov/solar/pv_basics.html (accessed 24 July 2008).

U.S. Department of the Interior. Bureau of Land Management. "Coal and Electricity Equivalents, 2001." http://www.blm.gov/ut/st/en/prog/energy/coal/electricity_conversion.html (accessed 28 August 2008).

U.S. Department of the Interior. Bureau of Reclamation. "Grand Coulee Dam Statistics and Facts." November 2007. http://www.usbr.gov/pn/grandcoulee/pubs/factsheet.pdf (accessed 11 August 2008).

U.S. Environmental Protection Agency. "Municipal Solid Waste Generation, Recycling, and Disposal in the United States: Facts and Figures for 2006." November 2007. http://www.epa.gov/garbage/pubs/msw06.pdf (accessed 28 July 2008).

Wertz, Richard R. *Special Report: Three Gorges Dam.* http://www.ibiblio.org/chinesehistory/contents/07spe/specrep01.html (accessed 10 August 2008).

Wisconsin K–12 Energy Education Program. "What Is Energy?" http://www.uwsp.edu/CNR/wcee/keep/Mod1/Whatis/energyresourcetables.htm (accessed 28 August 2008).

World Energy Council. "2007 Survey of Energy Resources." http://www.worldenergy.org/documents/ser2007_final_online_version_1.pdf (accessed 12 July 2008).

———. "2007 Survey of Energy Resources Executive Summary." http://www.worldenergy.org/documents/ser2007_executive_summary.pdf (accessed 12 July 2008).

World Health Organization. "Health Effects of the Chernobyl Accident and Special Health Care Programmes, 2006. http://

www.who.int/ionizing_radiation/chernobyl/who_chernobyl_
report_2006.pdf, p. 23 (accessed 14 November 2008).

World Nuclear Association. "Australia's Uranium and Nuclear
Power Prospects." September 2008. http://www.world-nuclear.
org/info/inf48.html (accessed 22 September 2008).

———. "Nuclear Power in France." May 2008. http://www.
world-nuclear.org/info/inf40.html (accessed 15 July 2008).

———. "World Nuclear Power Reactors 2007–08 and Uranium
Requirements." 8 August 2008. http://www.world-nuclear.
org/info/reactors.html (accessed 30 August 2008).

———. "World Uranium Mining." July 2008. http://world-
nuclear.org/info/inf23.html (accessed 14 November 2008).

World Wind Energy Association. "Wind turbines generate
more than 1% of the global electricity." Press release, 21 February 2008. http://www.wwindea.org/home/images/stories/
pr_statistics2007_210208_red.pdf (accessed 24 July 2008).

Index

Pages in **boldface** are illustrations.

About the Author

Ann Heinrichs is the author of more than 230 books for children and young adults on U.S. and world history and cultures, as well as science and nature, biographies, and grammar. For Marshall Cavendish Benchmark she has written *The Nile, The Sahara, The Amazon Rain Forest,* and *Mount Everest* in the Nature's Wonders series. She has also enjoyed successful careers as a children's book editor and an advertising copywriter. Born in Fort Smith, Arkansas, Heinrichs now lives in Chicago. An avid world traveler, she has toured Europe, East Asia, the Middle East, and Africa. For relaxation, she enjoys bike riding and kayaking.